Macaws ...getting started

Horst Schmidt

Contents

Photographs and illustration credits: David Alderton, Dr. Herbert R. Axelrod, Joan Balzarini, Cliff Bickford, William T. Cooper, Michael Defreitas, Isabelle Francais, Michael Gilroy, Ray Hansen, A.J. Mobbs, Horst Mueller, Dr. E.J. Mulawka, Paradise Park Hawaii, Robert Pearcy, San Diego Zoo, Ralph Small, Carol Thiem, L. van der Meid, Vogelpark Walsrode, Dr. Matthew Vriends

Originally published in German under the title *Die Aras* by Albrecht Philler Verlag, Minden, Copyright Albrecht Philler Verlag GmbH.

© T.F.H. Publications, Inc.

Distributed in the UNITED STATES to the Pet Trade by T.F.H. Publications, Inc., 1 TFH Plaza, Neptune City, NJ 07753; on the Internet at www.tfh.com; in CANADA by Rolf C. Hagen Inc., 3225 Sartelon St., Montreal, Quebec H4R 1E8; Pet Trade by H & L Pet Supplies Inc., 27 Kingston Crescent, Kitchener, Ontario N2B 2T6; in ENGLAND by T.F.H. Publications, PO Box 74, Havant PO9 5TT; in AUSTRALIA AND THE SOUTH PACIFIC by T.F.H. (Australia), Pty. Ltd., Box 149, Brookvale 2100 N.S.W., Australia; in NEW ZEALAND by Brooklands Aquarium Ltd., 5 McGiven Drive, New Plymouth, RD1 New Zealand; in SOUTH AFRICA by Rolf C. Hagen S.A. (PTY.) LTD., P.O. Box 201199, Durban North 4016, South Africa; in JAPAN by T.F.H. Publications. Published by T.F.H. Publications, Inc.
MANUFACTURED IN THE
UNITED STATES OF AMERICA
BY T.F.H. PUBLICATIONS, INC.

Introduction

In this book I am interested in providing the reader with insight into the classification of the macaw within the order Psittaciformes (parrots), describing the lives of these birds in their natural habitats in Central and South America, and describing the extinct species as is still possible.

Central to this book are the descriptions of individual species in the wild, their care in captivity and their breeding. Specific accounts of breeding attempts of the macaw in human care and successes there of are included in view of the fact that the captive breeding of this bird may be the only means of saving it from extinction—a responsibility to be considered seriously in our time.

Classification

In zoological classification, the following categories are used: order, family, sub-family, genus, and species. Within the zoological classification of Aves (birds) is the order Psittaciformes (parrots), a specific and distinct group. Based on anatomical similarities, parrots were originally grouped closely with the Joined-toed Cuckoo. Both bird classes were designated as having two toes facing the front and two facing backwards. In the *Check-List of Birds of the World*, written in 1937 by James Lee Peters, parrots are listed after pigeons, and before touracos, cuckoos, and owls. In 1964 Von

Red-fronted Macaw, *Ara rubrogenys*. In the wild, the Red-fronted macaw invades the peanut and corn fields and causes significant damage.

Boetticher suggested that the toe formation of the parrots and the cuckoos were a result of independent adaptation, and did not imply a relationship between the two. This book will use even more recent classifications following the work of Wolters (1975), who revised parts of the categories given by Bereton and Immelman (1962), and Forshaw (1973). Wolters divides the order Psittaciformes into 11 families. Within each species, sub-species are listed, which are presented under their respective genera (like Forshaw, 1973, omitting the extinct species).

The Blue-throated Macaw, *Ara glaucogularis*, was known up until recently as *Ara caninde*. It was given an individual status after a recent review of the living *Ara* species. In the species descriptions, the history of the names of these birds will be given. The author follows the proposal of Lantermann's, who concludes after intensive study of the old literature, "that the name *caninde* is a synonym for *ararauna*, and consequently should not be used, since it identifies this bird with the other known Blue and Yellow Macaw."

Therefore Lantermann claims, in his monograph *Macaws*, 1984, that the designating species name *glaucogularis* should be applied, as Dabenne first suggested in 1921, and which Hoppe also uses earlier.

THE EXTINCT SPECIES

Discussion of extinct Macaws creates an especially distressing chapter in a book of this nature. Included are one species from the genus *Anodorhynchus* and eight species from the genus *Ara*. Very little is known about the external descriptions of these birds. In Lord Rothschild's book *Extinct Birds* (1907), there are colored illustrations that he collected from the records of travelling naturalists and from some of the skins and feathers in museum collections.

SPECIES PROTECTION

Unscrupulous persecution and commercial capture largely affects the macaw species. The handling of captive birds, and their breeding, may in the long run contribute to the protection of the various species. In last decade there have been severe changes in the world ecology. Through clearing and

Hybrid. Scarlet Macaw, *Ara macao,* x Green Wing Macaw, *Ara chloroptera.* At one time, the Scarlet Macaw was considered very rare and was very difficult to attain. This being the case, it is not always wise to hybridize. If we breed species to prevent extinction, a considerable effort must be made not to hybridize.

industrialization, the majority of macaw species have been so disrupted that some are in direct danger of becoming extinct. Uncontrolled capture, exportation, and importation have contributed to the decline in their populations. Hoppe proposes in his work an extensive attempt to balance the world change: specifically, focusing on the constantly advancing and extensive exploitation of the tropical rain forests effected by the steady demand by European and North American industries for timber and precious woods. It is estimated "that the tropical rain forest can survive at the most three more years of uprooting, to produce lumber, before it becomes entirely karstic."

In the meantime, the birds will have lost all of the habitats and sustenance provided by the plants and trees, protection from the rain and sun, and nesting and roosting trees. Another factor in the rapid destruction of the forest vegetation has been the development of oil fields in the Amazon region. "For example, Brazil has lost huge areas of virgin forest in previous years to exploitation. By the end of the century, the macaw will have been completely driven out of their previously lush domain. The exploitation for mineral resources has also contributed to this end: oil, gold, silver, diamonds, iron, copper, tin, titanium, lead, uranium, nickel, bauxite, and coal." The following macaw species are listed in Appendum I of the March 3, 1973 Washington Species Protection Treaty. They are considered to be in direct danger of extinction: *Anodorhynchus glaucus*(Glaucous Macaw), *Anodorhynchus leari* (Lear's Macaw), and *Cyanopsitta spixii*(Spix's Macaw). All of the other macaw species are listed in the July 1, 1981 Appendum II. Appendum I forbids the trade of any bird listed therein. With the exception of scientific authorities— exhibiting special federal permits from the Office of Nutrition and Forestry— this excludes professional bird handling. Birds listed in Appendum II can be granted exportation, provided there has been scientific verification that the exportation of birds in this species will not endanger the survival of the species, when the federal protection laws are not broken in the process, and when humane exportation procedures are followed. As a result of the

Spix's Macaw, *Cyanopsitta spixii.* Spix's Macaw is considered extremely rare. There are only a few known breeding pairs throughout the world, and the hope of propagating the species is rare.

species protection conference held in Gaborone, Botswana, from April 19-April 30, 1983, on July 27, 1983, *A. glaucogularis* (Blue-throated Macaw), and *A. rubrogenys* (Red-fronted Macaw) have been added to Appendum I. Hoppe advocates that extreme measures must also be taken for the Hyacinth Macaw—*Anodorhynchus hyacinthinus*—by adding it to Appendum I as well. In addition: At the 5th Species Protection Conference held from April 22, to May 3, 1985, in Buenos Aires, the *Ara macao* (Scarlet Macaw) and the *Ara ambigua* (Buffon's Macaw) were both transferred from Appendum II to Appendum I, of the Washington Endangered Species Protection Treaty.

Macaw Species

HYACINTH MACAW

Scientific Name: *Anodorhynchus hyacinthinus*,Latham, 1790

Common Name: Hyacinth Macaw

Field Marks: 98-100 cm (39-40in)long; cobalt-blue, somewhat brighter on its head, sides of the neck and front; darker on the neck, rear and wings; black-blue undersides of the primary and secondary feathers, and tail feathers; eye ring and base of the lower mandible orange-yellow, deplumated skin area; beak gray-black; irises dark brown; feet gray-black. Females may be somewhat smaller. Immatures smaller than the adult males, and have shorter tail feathers.

Dissemination: Southern Brazil in Para, Bahia, Goias, Minas Gerais, Mato Grosso, south-western Piaui and southern Maranhao.

Range: Very little research has been conducted in this bird's natural habitat, even though its dissemination covers an area 1.5 million square kilometers (932,100 square miles), six times the total area of West Germany. The Hyacinth Macaw appears to prefer the highlands and mountainous regions, although they also can be found in the river basins, and have been documented along the Amazon, Paraguay, and Parana tributaries. They live in pairs in gallery forests, savannas, swamp forests, and palm groves. More

Four and one-half week old Blue and Gold Macaws, *Ara ararauna*. Baby Blue and Gold Macaws tend to grow right before your eyes. In another 6 weeks, these birds will be fully feathered and close to adult size.

Cage chains and bird seed guards are available at your local pet store. The cage chain can be used to suspend your bird's cage from the ceiling. Bird guards are very useful because they help to keep the mess that falls out of the cage to a minimum. Photo courtesy of Rolf C. Hagen Corp.

often the birds are seen in families of four to six birds. According to Lantermann they have also been documented living in flocks of 20 birds. Luckily there are some regions which the birds inhabit that are so inaccessible and out of the way that human development in the near future is not to be feared. Notably the swampy Panatal region in Paraguay provides a habitat that is still intact. Hoppe thinks it is possible that the Hyacinth Macaw has extended its range to the borders of Bolivia and even the edges of Paraguay.

The macaws search for food in the morning either in pairs or in small groups,

preferring the various palm species. They also feed on berries and seeds. With their strong beaks they have no problem opening even the hardest palm nuts. Observers have described their flight as "quick and impressive," with mates maintaining continual contact throughout flight. After eating, the birds rest silently in the tops of the trees, preening their feathers and feeding again intermittently. They scratch each other's plumage, thereby maintaining strong social contact.

In the late afternoons, the birds seek their roosting sites. Occasionally they are seen sitting with

other macaw species. This species generally uses old palm trees for its nest, preferring trunks of the Buriti Palm. The brood consists of two to three eggs, each measuring 53 x 35 mm (2.4x1.4in), and weighing 45g (1.5oz). The female bird clutches and warms the eggs alone in the first part of the brooding, with the male keeping a close guard. When the immatures are about 3 months old, they leave the nest, but are fed by the parents for another week.

Status: One can say without exaggeration that the Hyacinth Macaw is the most impressive of the large parrots. Its handsome colors, its tremendous statures, and powerful beak are singularly fascinating.

So great is the desire among parrot enthusiasts to own a Hyacinth Macaw that a number of problems in their upkeep must be unequivocally pointed out. First of all, it would hardly be ethical, in view of this species' prospects of survival through the next century, to keep solitary birds. It seems more fitting that they be kept in pairs with the intention of propagating the species. Secondly, one must consider the enormous stature of this bird;

Hyacinth Macaw, *Anodor-hynchus hyacinthinus,* with blocks. Not only are macaws playful, but they are intelligent too! Most are eager to learn to do tricks and mimic phrases.

ordinary parrot cages do not accommodate a bird of this size, nor would their structures survive the powerful beak of the Hyacinth Macaw. They have been known to tear down cement walls when no suitable gnawing material was present.

The birds should be kept in pairs in a sturdy aviary with a heated inner chamber. It should be at least 6 meters (19.7 feet) long to give the birds room to fly; with fencing made of a wavy grating with cables 4-5 mm (.16 - .23 in) thick and a 25 x 25 mm (1 x 1 in) mesh. In an aviary of this nature, the Hyacinth Macaw will quickly become tame, and develop a trusting attitude towards its keeper, although one must always be aware of its powerful beak. An aggressive or upset bird can easily bite through a human finger. Hoppe forecasts (1983) that mass exportation of this bird from South America will no longer be possible. Individual birds will be obtainable only from collections of captive birds, or from individuals in the trade. He therefore suggests: "It is to be feared that within a few years, the Hyacinth Macaw will have completely disappeared from the possession of bird enthusiasts since there have been few specialists able to breed new generations of this bird in captivity. Amateurs in possession of solitary birds should either seek a mate for the bird, or turn it over to a breeder. This is the only way it will be possible to maintain a small population of the Hyacinth Macaw in captivity in the future."

The first Hyacinth Macaw is presumed to have arrived in Europe in 1867 in the London Zoo. This bird was later exhibited at the Berlin Zoo, and in the Hagenbeck Zoo, in Hamburg around 1880. After 1970, large numbers of the Hyacinth Macaw were bought by zoos around the world. I saw an enormous swarm of this gorgeous blue bird in 1978, but wondered whether the cries of these captive birds were enthusiastic or sad.

There has been extensive observation of this bird in captivity both in the Wilhalmina Zoo in Stuttgart and in the Bochum Animal Park. The bird-handlers have been quite enthusiastic about the playfulness and trusting nature of this spectacular macaw, although they have seen no signs of extraordinary talent in their speaking aptitudes. They are, however, quite agile, and the trainers at Bird Jungle, Miami, have taught the members of this species some wonderful acrobatic maneuvers that have been known to endlessly amuse spectators. Breeding attempts, documented since around 1960, indicate that under proper conditions, the Hyacinth Macaw is not a difficult bird to breed. The first success was recorded at the Kobe Zoo in Japan. A single chick hatched there while at around the same time a brood of five eggs hatched at the Chicago Zoo. These five were hand-raised because the parents refused to feed the chicks. One year later a pair was bred in the Bratislava Zoo in Czechoslovakia; the hatchling died two weeks after birth. This pair did not breed again until 1978. After a number of futile attempts, a pair of Hyacinth Macaws in Brookfield (U.S.A.) produced a total of four immatures in the years 1972 and 1973. The female laid her first egg when she was about 19 years old, and the male 13. Decoteau writes in 1982 that there have been many successful pairings in the U.S.A. in private handling. An amateur in Ohio writes of having raised a number of

young birds with a warmed paste of shelled and ground sunflower seeds, oatmeal and ground carrots, with suitable vitamins and minerals added. The Houston Zoo also hand-raised some young birds in 1975.

The first European breeding almost happened in 1981 in the Walsrode Zoo; the only egg laid was destroyed by the parents. This pair lived in an aviary measuring 6 x 2.5 x 2.5 meters (19.5 x 8 x 8 feet) with a nest situated 80 cm (31.5 in.) above the ground. The nest was 40 cm (15.51 in.) in diameter, its entrance was 12 cm (4.7 in.) in diameter. The birds' behavior changed markedly before and after the egg was dropped. Before the egg was laid "the female silently disappeared into the nest with the male clinging to and thus securing the entrance." (Lantermann, 1984.) After the egg was laid, the female went into the nest only when there was some kind of disturbance. When the male exited the nest he typically stood before the entrance swinging his head. Shortly before the female dropped her egg, the bare spot of skin on her beak turned from a yellow-orange to a pale yellow. G. Volkemer of Frankfurt

Pair of Illiger's Macaws, *Ara maracana*. Macaws are avid wood chewers as seen from the condition of this tree.

received quite a bit of attention from the bird world when he reported his successful breeding in *The Feathered World, Vol. 1,* 1985. In 1977 he purchased a pair of birds but was dismayed to receive only one bird in his shipment. These birds were kept in an aviary measuring 4 m (13 feet) long, 2 m (8.2 ft.) high, and 1.5 m (5 ft.) wide. It had an enclosed chamber 1.75 m (5.5 ft.) long, 2 m (8.2 ft.) high and 1.5 m (5 ft.) wide. The birds did not seem sensitive to the cold temperatures in the winter months, even in the frost, however, the temperature did not drop below 0°C (32°F). Their nest was made of a light wood and measured 1 m (3.3 ft.) high and 50 cm (20 in.) in diameter, its entrance was 20 cm (8 in.) in diameter. The original report provides a solid lesson in the breeding of the Hyacinth Macaw: "I installed metal panels in all of the corners of the nest in order to prevent the birds from destroying the nest. I attached oak branches around the entrance, to give it a more natural appearance, and to make natural wood available to the birds for biting, hoping they'd do less damage to the structure. I also placed

rotted and broken pieces of wood on the floor of the nest." The pair fed on fruit, dried bark, and veal bones, a mixture of corn, oats, wheat, hemp, sunflower seeds, and peanuts, complemented with feeding chalk, minerals, mussel shells, and a multivitamin that was given for five consecutive days every four weeks. The breeder also observed that the pair swallowed small stones 1 - 4 mm (.04 - .16 in.) to aid their digestion.

When the birds started their breeding period in the end of May, 1982, the female entered the nest, and both birds were very defensive towards humans that approached the nest.

After 30 days of brooding, the female clutched the eggs alone. A single chick hatched. The other egg that had been laid disappeared after 14 days. Volkemer wrote that the egg measured 50 x 35 mm (1.97 x 1.38 in.) and weighed 20g (.64 oz.).

Volkemer described the development of the immatures: "During the first week of life the young birds emitted soft sounds, but after that they were quiet until they had learned to imitate the shrieks of the parents. They opened their eyes after 14 days. In addition to the feed described above, I also offered them sprouted wheat and oats, sunflower seeds and corn, and unripe cobs of corn. After three months, a perfectly feathered Hyacinth emerged from the nest, nearly the size of its parents. It was distinguishable from its parents primarily by its somewhat brighter and yellower eye ring, and its plumage had a darker shine." This same pair raised another two birds and the breeder raised another bird a year later with a different pair.

In the same issue of that journal, J. Steinbacher mentions an article in a Frankfurt newspaper from October 10, 1984, about a bird living in a glass enclosure in a large zoo in Frankfurt that raised a young bird out of a litter of

Two Hyacinth Macaws, *Anodorhynchus hyacinthinus*. These two macaws have their eyes set on biting into this branch. A piece of wood this size could easily be destroyed by any macaw.

three eggs. The most recent article comes from an article in the *Poultry Exchange*, July 1985. A two year old female Hyacinth Macaw mated with a Blue and Gold Macaw and laid her eggs in the living room of the breeder. She made her nest behind a small stereo stand, and furnished it with record covers, the veneer from cabinets, and pieces of wallpaper. Unfortunately her eggs were destroyed—one had apparently been brooded, and contained an approximately 10-day-old embryo. With much idealism the enthusiast wrote: "Fourteen days later the new cupboards came, the aviary came a day later, and until its completion,

the pair quietly and completely destroyed the old walls of the apartment. "We were subsequently occupied with the building of the room-aviary, when from under the coffee-table,

which had also been demolished, the birds began a frontal attack on us: biting, shrieking, snarling, growling, etc. The room was again destroyed, which I don't mind: the two could destroy all of the furniture as long as they are breeding. Five days later, I found a disorderly nest with three eggs of recognizable size and color. The nest was made of pieces of carpeting, door, frames, video cassettes, and various pieces of plastic, which were later identified as light switches and the color tuning knob of the television set." Unfortunately the female quit her clutch 16 days later, the nest and the eggs were destroyed. This idealist remarks conclusively: "In the meantime the pair was put in the large aviary, and I finally got the wall replaced. Furniture and renovations cost me approximately $2500 dollars! This brood failed at a ridiculous cost: Next time it'll succeed!"

GLAUCOUS MACAW

Scientific Name: *Anodorhynchus glaucus*, Vieillot, 1816

Common Name: Glaucous Macaw

Field Marks: 72 cm (28.35 in) long; general plumage greenish-blue; head and neck more grayish than blue; throat, cheeks and upper breast gray-brownish overlaid; under side more greenish; under side of the tail feathers brownish; eye ring and side of the beak and cere bare and yellow; irises dark brown; beak black, with a gray tip; feet dark brown to black. Differences between the sexes and the immatures are unknown.

Dissemination: It is presently not known whether the Glaucous Macaw still lives in its original habitat. Available literature agrees that it is

Military Macaw, *Ara militaris*. A Military Macaw may not be as colorful as the other species, but it is a very playful bird in its own right.

Caninde Macaw, *Ara caninde*. This macaw is very similar to the Blue and Gold Macaw. However, it is rarely seen in captivity.

extremely rare. Its territory is quoted as follows: Central and southern Paraguay; southwestern Mato Grosso in Brazil; northeastern Argentina and possibly in northwestern Uruguay and in the western part of Rio Grande do Sul in Brazil.

Range: Naturalists searching for this elusive bird in past years have come up empty-handed, causing many ornithologists to believe it to be extinct. Hoppe considered this premature: in late fall of 1982 he received information that a Bolivian animal handler had Glaucous Macaws in his possession. The reports were not consistent, however. Supposedly the Glaucous Macaw lives in the swamp areas of the Paraguayan rivers, where it should exist in very small numbers.

Lantermann writes that the last wild Glaucous Macaw was observed in northeastern Argentina in 1960. Nothing is known of their breeding; it is presumed to mate between October and January/ February. In 1982 research was contradictory: Low claimed that the species was indeed extinct, and Decoteau calculated a small remaining population in Uruguay.

The species observed in northwestern Uruguay and reported by DeGrahl in 1962 was never verified. The beautiful sea-blue bird first reached the London Zoo in 1860, eight years later in Amsterdam and in Hamburg/Hagenbeck in 1878 according to Russ. Decoteau believes there are some in private collections in Europe, possibly even to this day. "This animal feeds on a paste of turkey-breeding feed, curds and small seeds, which freshly prepared, can be fed twice a day." (Lantermann, 1984.) Understandably the possession of pairs of this bird is kept secret. At any rate, there are thought to have been a large number of young birds raised in the past years. The length of the fledgling period is 120 days. Hoppe believes he saw two Glaucous Macaws a few years ago in the possession of an animal trader, but failed to recognize them as such at the time. This leads me to believe that this rare species may often be mistaken by importers as immature Hyacinth Macaws. A Dutch or Belgian bird park was thought to have a Glaucous Macaw in the late 1970's. And finally, a verified account was recorded by Haberland in a 1928 book, *Birds of Distant Lands*

Blue and Gold Macaw, *Ara ararauna*. The Blue and Gold must be the most favorable of the macaws. They are the most playful and are attractive as well.

Noble Macaw, *Diopsittaca nobilis*. Macaws usually pair bond for life. If a bonded pair is separated and matched with another mate, chances are the new mate will not be accepted.

(Magdeburg), in which he quotes the Dutch bird handler Blazer as having seen a Glaucous Macaw in the Rotterdam Zoo. This species is fully protected under Appendum I of the Washington Endangered Species Treaty.

LEAR'S MACAW

Scientific Name: *Anodorhynchus leari*, Bonaparte, 1856

Field Marks: 75 cm (29.53 in) long; primarily dark blue with greenish overlay; underside more gray (Pinter); top side of wings and tail cobalt blue; underside of tail dark grayish-blue; according to De Grahl the shoulder feathers and wing coverts have bright feather edgings; skin around eyes and on base of the beak unfeathered and yellowish (brighter than on the Hyacinth Macaw!); beak dark gray to black; irises brown; feet gray-black. Color and size distinctions between the sexes and of the immatures are unknown.

Some ornithologists believe the Lear's Macaw to be a bastard of the *A. hyacinthinus* and *A. glaucus*, others consider it to be a sub-species of *A. glaucus*. Research done by Prof. Sick established this bird as a separate species in 1978.

Dissemination: Eastern Brazil (Pernambuco and Bahia provinces).

Range: This species is considered by scientists to be among the rarest birds on earth. Its natural habitat has been researched little. Sick saw 21 individual birds flying in Raso do Catarina, north Bahia and was able to inspect their roosting and nesting areas. He writes: "On my birthday, January 10, 1969, I found myself in a canyon which is often frequented by macaws, and observed at least 15 birds as they returned to their roost. This was accomplished with my new telescope that was delivered to me a few days before my departure on a research grant in the Brazilian province of Bahia. It was the culmination of a year-long struggle to import this equipment from the Ost-Zeiss. The telescope's sight exactly encompassed a pair of these proud birds (without the long tails). They were surrounded by a swarm of birds flying into the trees and scratched themselves nervously on the head. It was certainly the most memorable birthday of my life." For this discovery Prof. Sick and his student Dante M. Teixeira received the Brazilian gold medal from the 1st Ibero-American Ornithologists Congress in Buenos Aires. Sick

wrote in 1983 that while a guard is being hired, the few remaining Lear's Macaws must clearly be guarded. It is agreed that one specimen must be killed for scientific purposes and rushed to the National Museum, Rio de Janeiro, to be prepared and studied. Hoppe mentions yet another isolated bird displayed by the city of Santo Antao in the Pernambuco province. The bird was found in the Juazeiro region along the left bank of San Francisco.

Outside of their natural habitat, no recorded observations of their breeding behavior

Caninde Macaw, *Ara caninde*, and Blue and Gold, *Ara ararauna*. The entire upperparts of the Caninde Macaw, including the forehead and forecrown, are blue, paler and more greenish than the Blue and Gold.

Hyacinth Macaw, *Anodor-hynchus hyacinthinus.* Macaws are very valuable pets, both in personality as well as monetary value. Should your bird appear listless or change its behavior in any negative way, consult your veterinarian immediately.

exists. One Lear's Macaw was found accidentally among a transport of Hyacinth Macaws. However, the Brazilian government has effected a general ban on any handling of this bird for a number of years now.

In the 1800's, the London Zoo had a specimen of the Lear's Macaw living in its bird house. An egg of this bird's was carefully preserved and is kept today in the collection of the British Museum of Natural History, where it is a closely guarded treasure. It measures 75 x 38.4 mm (3 x 1.5 in.).

Single birds of this species have been kept in the past in the zoos in San Diego, Los Angeles, and Brookfield in the USA and also in Copenhagen, Basel, and Walsrode. A pair of birds in the Basel Zoo was documented as having bred. In 1983 there was only one adult left; since then a young bird, raised in captivity and another adult bird have been brought in. In the 19th century solitary Lear's Macaws were taken into London (1880), Berlin (1883), and Hamburg (1893), (De Grahl, 1974). According to Decoteau, (1982) in the cities of San

Diego, Miami, and Tampa there were a total of 11 birds. It is not known whether there are other birds of this species in existence—perhaps in Europe.

Hoppe has received a personal communication from T. Silva of Tampa-Bush Gardens, Florida, that in July 1982, a young Lear's Macaw hatched. To insure its safety, this chick was raised by hand. With another mating, the pair—nearly 30 years old—produced another young bird (September, 1982). Dr. J.M. Lernould, Director of Parc Zoologique et Botanique in Mulhouse, France, believes there to be two Lear's Macaws in France—one in the private sector, another in the Menagerie in Paris. This is not yet confirmed.

Lear's Macaw is a fully protected species under Appendum I of the Washington Species Protection Act. Prepared skins can be found in the Senckenberg Museum in Frankfurt and in the Paris Museum.

SPIX'S MACAW
Scientific Name: *Cyanopsitta spixii*,Wagler, 1832

Illustration: Spix's Macaw is the only species within the genus *Cyanopsitta*.

It is distinguished from the neighboring genus *Anodorhynchus* by the dark gray skin of the unfeathered area around the eyes and on the base of the beak. The facial area is otherwise completely feathered—like the genus *Ara*. In 1964 Von Boetticher classified Spix's Macaw as an *Ara*; Forshaw (1973), and Wolters (1975) established the genus *Cyanopsitta*.

Field Marks: 56 cm (22 in) long; general plumage cobalt blue; more gray-blue on the head, cheeks and ear patch; neck and breast grayish green-blue; bare gray eye region and lore stripes; underside of the tail feathers dark gray; beak gray-black; feet dark gray.

Immatures have a darker general plumage; the tail feathers are shorter and their beaks have horn colored specks.

Dissemination: Eastern Brazilian provinces of Piaui, Panagua, northern Bahia and possibly Maranhao.

Range: Spix's Macaw was discovered in 1820 by Dr. J.B.V. Spix in eastern Brazil. Spix toured Brazil with the Botanist C.F.P. Martius and brought a prepared skin to the

Museum in Munich. The young zoologist, Prof. J.G. Wagler, scientifically described the newly discovered macaw in 1832 and named it after its discoverer.

It was next observed in 1903 by Reiser in the province of Panagua. Since then there have been no verified instances of sightings in their natural habitat. Hoppe described the habitat: "Spix's Macaw lives in the mountainous region of northern Brazil. The climate there is tropical; precipitation is occasional, breaking up lengthy dry periods. The vegetation in the Caatinge dry region is suited to the lack of rainfall, yielding an arid bush country. The river regions have some gallery forests and swampy forests."

Spix's Macaw seems well adapted to this region but is rarely seen in its own habitat as is true with the Glaucous and Lear's Macaws.

Hoppe suggests that "the extreme climatic conditions in the Caatinga region would account for the scarcity of individuals of any species." Because of the long distances that Spix's Macaw often must fly, they are difficult to study. Despite DeSchauensee's reports of Spix's Macaws inhabiting palm groves (1970), it is not certain that he had studied them in the wild. They most likely prefer gallery forests crossed with shrub forests. They may not have regular breeding seasons but may breed depending on the rains and the availability of food.

The London Museum of Natural History has eggs measuring 35 x 29 mm (1.5 x 1 in). It also has a stuffed skin of this species, as does the Senckenberg Museum, Frankfurt am Main.

Spix's Macaw, *Cyanopsitta spixii*, is a very rare bird about which little is known.

Status: The first Spix's Macaw arrived in Europe in the Berlin Zoo in 1893; Lantermann writes of one 17 years earlier in London. According to DeGrahl, a Dr. Burgess was in possession of a female in 1924, who was later to drop one egg. The Paignton Zoo in England kept a pair around 1927. Another pair was exhibited at the 1965 World's Fair in Rotterdam, the female of which laid an egg on this momentous occasion! K. Plath from Illinois (1928) kept a young Spix's Macaw that was very tame and an able talker. Unfortunately this bird was placed in a zoo in 1946 with two amazons, who killed him.

There are presently individuals of this

Catalina Macaw. In the wild, it has been recorded that natural cross breedings have taken place between the Scarlet Macaw and the Blue and Gold Macaw.

handsome blue species being kept in American zoos, in Neapal, and by an unnamed Belgian bird enthusiast. The late Yugoslavian leader Tito was also known to have a bird of this species in his parrot collection. Its fate is unknown.

Decoteau, in his 1982 volume *Handbook of Macaws* (T.F.H. Publishers, Neptune, NJ), accounts for at least three pairs of this rare bird in the U.S.A. and

Belgium. He mentions Germany but with no further accounts; presumably he is referring to the macaws in the Walsrode Bird Park. Also in recent years, breeding of this species has been successful. A Belgian pair produced 18 young birds between the years of 1976 and 1981. In 1979 two Spix's Macaws were bought for roughly $11,000 US dollars in England. There are also two specimens in a zoo in Rio de Janeiro. Dr. H. Strunden writes of them: "Both birds were quite lively in their large enclosure with their behavior ranging considerably from reciprocal preening to raucous arguments, in which the weaker of the two would finally fall to the floor of the cage and lying on its back try to defend its skin and feathers from the other bird with its beak and feet, shrieking loudly all the while."

The two Spix's Macaws that were brought to Walsrode in 1975 soon established themselves as mates. They were being hand-fed by their keepers in as few as two months. Unfortunately the male died in 1978 just as he was beginning his courting rituals. In 1982, Walsrode procured another pair of birds, so hopes of breeding still exist. There have also been breeding attempts in the Neapal Zoo since 1980. Hoppe has maintained communication with the bird keeper of that zoo, Mrs. Wenner, who writes: "The first egg was dropped in the nest. The second lay broken under the climbing stand. The first egg was

destroyed a short time later in the nest. In 1981 the female laid yet another two eggs, which lay broken, as in the previous years, among the gravel flooring. Hopefully 1982 will be a successful year. It will be wonderful, when it finally comes to pass, to have bred more of these rare birds."

Should these birds not be bred successfully at least in captivity, it is to be feared that the handsome Spix's Macaw will disappear from the aviaries of the world. This may be the last opportunity to help this species that is so severely threatened in its natural habitat.

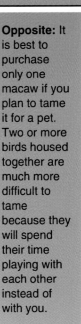

Opposite: It is best to purchase only one macaw if you plan to tame it for a pet. Two or more birds housed together are much more difficult to tame because they will spend their time playing with each other instead of with you.

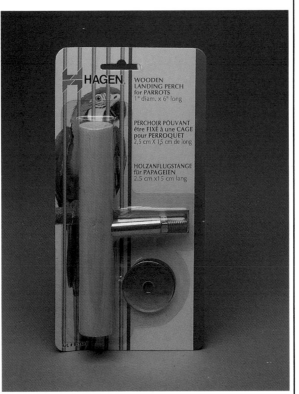

HAGEN WOODEN LANDING PERCH for PARROTS 1" diam. x 6" long

PERCHOIR POUVANT être FIXÉ à une CAGE pour PERROQUET 2,5 cm X 15 cm de long

HOLZANFLUGSTANGE für PAPAGEIEN 2.5 cm x15 cm lang

Left: A landing perch is a useful product; it easily attaches to the top of the bird's cage and allows it to sit for hours unconfined. Photo courtesy of Rolf C. Hagen Corp.

THE GENUS ARA

Twelve living species belong to this genus. The smallest measures 38 cm (15 in.), the largest 90 cm (35.5 in.). All of the macaws of this genus have either fully nude or partially feathered faces. Their tail feathers are graduated. The species listed in "Extinct Species," with the exception of the Cuban Macaw, whose existence has been documented, are only theoretically listed under this genus.

BLUE AND GOLD MACAW

Scientific Name: *Ara ararauna*, Linne, 1758

Common Name: Blue and Gold Macaw, and Yellow Breasted Macaw

Field Marks: 80-90 cm (31.5 - 35.5 in.)long; top side and long tail feathers medium blue; sides of the

Blue and Gold Macaw, *Ara ararauna*. All macaws have the potential for speech, some will talk better than others. Once a bird learns to talk, it continues to do so because of the extra attention it receives from performing.

Blue and Gold Macaw, *Ara ararauna*. Macaws require an enormous amount of space to exercise, both in and out of their housing facility. Their enormous body length coupled with their equally as long or longer tail usually requires a specially designed cage.

neck and entire underside deep yellow to yellow-orange; forehead and front of the head olive-green; the bare facial skin has three lines of small black feathers extending from the base of the upper mandible to the front of the ear region; between the eyes and beak run five or six vertical stripes of small feathers; the lower half of the face is entirely unfeathered; an olive-green to black band runs from the ear region over the throat; the undersides of the wings are olive-yellow; the beak is gray-black; feet dark gray; claws black; the adult birds have yellow irises; the immature's are more brownish. Immatures are somewhat smaller than the adults and have a washed-out look to their plumage; their beaks become dark after about two weeks. The females seem to be a bit smaller than the males.

Dissemination: Eastern Panama to Ecuador, possibly northern Peru; Southern Brazil to Bolivia, Paraguay, and supposedly also northern Argentina.

Until recently, the Blue-throated Macaw, earlier known as the Caninde Macaw, *A. glaucogularis*, was classified as a sub-species of *A. ararauna* (De Grahl, 1974). The newest research (Ingels, 1981 and

Blue and Gold Macaw, *Ara ararauna*. Macaws are natural acrobats and may learn a number of physical tricks. Some of the more physical tricks include rolling over, lying on their back, and playing dead.

Reinhard, 1982) indicates an individual species. Hoppe considers it possible that it is indeed a sub-species of *A. ararauna* on the basis of the varying intensities of yellow to orange respectively of the undersides of birds in northwestern South America as to the markings of those in the southern region of this bird's dissemination. The northernmost seem to be noticeably larger and stouter.

Range: The Blue and Gold Macaw always seems to live in river basins and in swamps. The presence of this imposing creature depends on the availability of food. They roam widely; their commute between roosting and feeding areas can measure up to 25 km (15.5 miles). In Bolivia they are often seen in the company of the Scarlet

Macaw, *A. macao*, and the Blue-throated Macaw, *A. glaucogularis*. The large bird finds sustenance in palm groves-mainly the Buriti palm: ripe and unripe fruit, also berries, nuts and different buds, leaves, and bark. They prefer the following palm species: *Mauritia*, *Oreodoxa*, *Astrocaryum*, *Bactris* and *Maximilianea*. They also use seeds from the Hura crepitans to aid in their digestion.

Forested river basins, and areas of the lowlands, swamps, and forests that have large overhanging trees are popular with Blue and Gold Macaws. They are seen in pairs during the breeding season, otherwise in large swarms. They are believed to be extinct in Paraguay and exist only in small numbers on the island of Trinidad. In 1959, French saw groups of up to about 15 birds. Hoppe fears the extinction of this bird on Trinidad within a few years. He predicts that nest-robbing will be 80% responsible for the castrophe. It is very easy to locate this animal during its flight, their loud calls make the nesting sites easy to find, and it is a simple matter to remove the young birds from the nest. This author was able to find many of these birds being kept by local parrot enthusiasts and bird handlers. "However: the

Blue and Gold Macaw, *Ara ararauna* eating Banana. As special treats, macaws enjoy a variety of fresh fruits and vegetables.

primary danger remains–
the changes happening
the world over have
disturbed the natural
balances."

During the day, Blue and
Gold Macaws search for
food. Taking off from their
roosting sites, the swarms
of birds let loose ear-
deafening shrieks. They
return again to their roosts
in late afternoon. Their
noise can be heard for
great distances as they sit
up to 100 birds together in
the trees.

They generally make
their nests in the holes of
dead palm trees. Pairs in
the northernmost areas
begin to breed in the
months of February/
March. In southern Brazil,
it begins in December/
January. Eggs have been
found as early as mid-
November in northern
Paraguay—the
southernmost extent of
their range. The female
clutches two to four eggs
for 27 days. From the
dropping of the second egg
on, the female remains
constantly on her eggs.
Both parents participate in
the feeding of the young
birds, which can last up to
three months. When the
immatures come out of the
nest they are immediately
astonishingly good, steady
fliers; they are
distinguished from the

parents only by their
shorter tail feathers. Little
by little the entire family
becomes integrated into the
large, gregarious swarms.

Status: The Blue and
Gold Macaw is not only the
most common macaw
species in Europe, North
America and Asia, it is
treasured throughout
South America as a
domesticated pet. It is
known to have a very
sociable nature, to be easily
tamed and very trusting,
and has beautiful plumage,
and is therefore the most
desirable of large parrots. It
has also been praised by
bird enthusiasts for its
speaking abilities.

In my guide book
*Speaking and Imitative
Birds*, I further discuss this
bird's aptitude for
imitating. The birds with
higher intelligence seem to
need quite a bit of attention
and understanding from
their keepers. Lantermann
is of the same opinion: "If
for nothing else than for
the protection of this
species, a bird enthusiast
considering buying a bird
of this nature should be
quite conscious of the
needs of these animals and
the obligations and
commitments they imply.
This bird is not suitable for
individuals with their
interior decoration in mind
or those that desire the

Opposite:
Blue and
Gold
Macaw, *Ara
ararauna.*
Upon
hatching, a
baby macaw
has dark
eyes that
progressively
get lighter as
the bird
matures.
When the
bird is about
one year old
the coloring
around the
iris changes
to white, and
an extremely
old bird will
have yellow
coloring.

flare of exotic creatures."

The Blue and Gold Macaw becomes even closer to its keeper during its reproductive years: the keeper becomes both surrogate mate and playmate. Most birds of this species are really very playful. They have been found to be quite compatible with birds of their own and other large parrot species. Information regarding their handling, feeding, and care can be found in their respective chapters.

It is relatively easy to breed the *Ara ararauna.* As early as 1921, K. Neunzig gave accounts of successful matings in his book entitled *Handbook for Bird Enthusiasts.* The first was accomplished in Caen, France sometime between 1818 and 1822, in which 19 pairs mated, and 25 young birds were produced. In three and a half years one female was recorded as having laid 62 eggs. Astonishingly, the pair raised 15 young birds in captivity. In 1892 there was also an alleged brood in France, and in 1894 H. Sharland recorded one in Belgium.

Other breeding attempts and raisings: 1901 in Czechoslovakia (two eggs, one young bird); 1932, Essen Animal Park, and other young birds produced under the auspices of M.T. Padbury in western Australia; 1933/34 Mrs. E.T. Stotesbury, U.S.A. (one bird); 1934 the first recorded breeding in England (Essex), and Germany (Essen); 1939, Sheffler, U.S.A.; 1939 Edinburgh Zoo (three eggs, two young birds, although only one achieved adulthood); 1948, Hallstrom, U.S.A.; 1958 Chessington Zoo, England, and by A. Larsen, Randers, Denmark; 1965 in Rode, England in the Tropical Bird Gardens; 1972, R. Kirchhofer hand-raised a brood in Switzerland; 1981 by Veser, Tettnang (Germany).

The informative account given by Hoppe of Veser's pair gives some basic information about the course and conditions of the Blue and Gold Macaw brood:

"In 1976 a pair of birds thought to be about 17 years old was procured; the animals originally came from Colombia. The birds were lodged in a double-barred inner aviary measuring 2.6 x 1.2 x 2 to 2.5 m (8.5 x 4 x 6.5 to 8 ft.) high and an outer aviary measuring 4 x 1.2 x 1.8 m (13 x 4 x 6 ft.) high. The only marks by which the hen and cock can be differentiated is the cock's wider, longer and darker tail, and the smaller size of the hen."

In 1978 the birds first became interested in the nest-hole constructed inside the inner aviary; the female laid fertilized eggs in March, which had unfortunately been damaged and died. Again in 1979 the breeding failed: despite extreme care regarding drafts, water seemed to have been blown into the nest. After yet another loss in 1980, the 1981 pairing produced a fertilized egg, and a young bird.

Hoppe describes the early stages of the bird's development: "On its first day of life it already had white downy feathers along its lower back, and a few as well on its head. The chick weighed 69 g (2.2 oz.) after 14 days. By this time all of the downy feathers had been shed, and the quills of its first feathers had begun to poke through the skin. In its first week of life, the male still fed only the female, after that it fed the young bird as well. After its 20th day its feathering was growing quickly. Its flying and steering feathers, as well as the feathers on its head grew faster than the other feathers. After 55 days, the tail feathers

Baby Blue and Gold Macaw, *Ara ararauna*. Young Blue and Gold Macaws can be hand fed with a syringe that has the needle removed. It is important to wipe the bird clean from any mush that may have splattered around its face.

measured about 10 cm (4 in.) long, and the chick weighed approximately 1100 g (35 oz.). On the 12th of October, three months after it hatched, the immature flew out of the nest weighing 1000 g (32 oz.). The immature was fed by its parents for yet another three months, despite its independence.

In the spring of 1985, the breeder Lothar Musial, in the vicinity of my own home, in Frankenhein, Schwalm-Ederkreis, produced a litter of eggs from a pair of Blue and Gold Macaws. After laying the first egg the female became lethargic and was placed in a separate cage. The second egg was noticeably smaller than the first. Both eggs were placed in an incubator for safety. It became apparent after a week of incubation that neither egg had been fertilized.

The breeder placed two Eclectus Parrot eggs under the macaw hen, and she clutched them for 30 days. In the last day of her clutch, one egg was broken, and the other was cast from the nest. After two more weeks, the female laid yet another two eggs and brooded the new clutch for another 30 days. One of these eggs was discovered missing one day, and the other egg was found to contain a fully-formed embryo which inexplicably did not hatch. It was observed that the shell had not been pecked at at all, leaving researchers to believe that either the chick had died just before trying to hatch, or had found the shell too hard and had not been able to break it open. This egg was also cast out of the nest.

After two consecutive failures to breed, the birds at first increased their breeding behavior; they became increasingly aggressive, and defensive of their nest, until the behavior ceased all at once. After a few weeks, when their molting began, their breeding urges stopped.

According to the breeder's accounts in 1976, the male was clearly recognizable as an immature, because of its dark irises. The female appeared to be more mature. In 1983 the male was observed feeding the female for the first time; he was thought to be seven years old. With this in mind, the pair does give hope for successful broods in the future.

De Grahl also writes of an unfertilized litter by a six-year-old pair in Rode, England. The following excerpt was found in a

German newspaper: "In Stotesbura, Palm Beach, in a volary filled with more than 60 birds, including six pairs of Green-winged Macaws, cockatiels and others, a pair of Blue and Gold Macaws have managed to breed successfully." The same author names the following feeds, which can be given to mating birds: sunflower seeds, various types of nuts, apples, pears, plums, grapes, oranges, tomatoes, egg-feed, soaked bread, cooked corn, biscuits, buds, bark, and coconuts.

The temporary rose-red cheek coloring has been variously thought of as a sex distinction, and/or an indication of a bird in its reproduction years. Lantermann has found both males and females with this mark, as well as newly fledged immatures, as has Kirchhofer of Switzerland.

On the 20th of August, 1985 I was able to observe a young Blue and Gold

Blue and Gold, *Ara ararauna* eating potato. The dietary requirements of macaws are extensive. You must provide ample amounts of fresh fruit and vegetables in addition to a good quality seed mixture.

Macaw, shortly before it was able to fly, in the Frankfurt Zoo. At that time, the glass enclosure had been built, housing a number of young macaws, but the curtain material, hung in front of the glass to keep the birds from crashing, had not yet been installed. The parents were being housed in a part of the outer aviary with some Scarlet Macaws. Obviously the breeding of the Blue and Gold Macaw was not disrupted by the presence of the different species.

The heads and beaks of the immatures are noticeably larger than those of the adult birds. And the darker irises are quite distinct. The tail feathers are only half as long as those of the fully grown birds. The young bird quietly climbed along the stands and nibbled playfully on the thin branches that were handed to him. He really made a singular impression.

Hybrids between *A. ararauna* and other *Ara* species are relatively common. Two young birds were raised in the Krefelder Zoo in 1973, parented by a Blue and Gold Macaw and a Scarlet Macaw. G. and O. Amme of Bissendorf, Germany, raised a young bird from a Blue and Gold and a Green-winged Macaw.

The Zoological Garden in Wupertal has the most productive pair of macaws known: since 1983 the Blue and Gold Macaw and its Green-winged mate have produced some 40 offspring, which have been in turn mated, though without results: the embryos have not survived.

M. Meier of Horgen, Switzerland, has also raised young birds from a similar pair. The name "Paradise

A number of different types of medications can be purchased from the pet store. Photo courtesy of Rolf C. Hagen Corp.

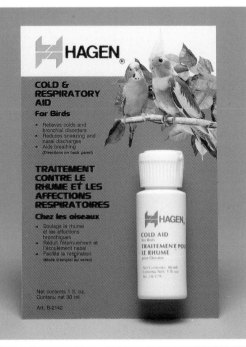

Macaw" has been rejected by scientists as a name for these birds, as have the names of either of their parents, since the offspring do not contribute to the maintenance of the original species.

Hybrids have also been produced from matings of the Blue and Gold Macaw with Buffon's Macaw and the Military Macaws (*A. ambigua* and *A. militaris*). Low (1980) writes of successful mating between *A. ararauna* and *A. hyacinthinus*. Lastly there have been matings between two birds of different genera.

Color deviations in the *ararauna* species are relatively rare. The Bleil family has written of immatures with brown/black plumage on the top side, and a white-breasted *ararauna* is known to live at the Zoological Garden in Branquilla, Colombia (Hoppe, 1983).

BLUE-THROATED MACAW

Scientific Name: *Ara glaucogularis*, Dabenne, 1921, earlier known as *Ara caninde*, Wagler, 1832

Field Marks: 75 cm (30 in.) long (Hoppe), 85 cm (34 in.) long (De Grahl and Lantermann); topside blue with green-blue shimmer along the forehead and front of the head (medium blue on

Catalina Macaw bathing. Macaws require a large vessel to bathe in. Whatever is used should be heavy enough so that it does not tip over; a ceramic dish is usually best.

ararauna!); blue wings; orange-yellow under side; under tail coverts blue; under side of tail feathers orange-yellow; as opposed to the *A. ararauna*, *A. glaucogularis* has a smaller cheek area, which has thicker plumage. Its facial plumage is a brighter green than that of the Blue and Yellow; its throat patch is dark blue and more in the shape of a bib; a thin yellow-orange stripe runs from in front of the ear coverts to the shoulder; beak black-gray; toes brown/black to dark gray; irises are yellowish-white in the adult birds, brownish in the immature birds. Sexual distinctions in appearance are unknown; immatures have smaller bodies.

Up until 17 years after it was first classified, *A. glaucogularis* was thought to be a sub-species of *A. ararauna*. (Low, 1972, and De Grahl, 1974). Dabenne was the first to differentiate the species from *A. ararauna* in 1921. Hoppe has substantiated Dabenne's work in recent years, having examined more than ten specimens. These authors consider the following qualities to be central to this distinction: different feather patterns along the facial skin (specifically: *A.*

glaucogularis has four narrowly spaced rows of feathers while *A. ararauna* has three, more broadly spaced); also: "*A. glaucogularis* has plumage extending from its forehead centrally to the base of its beak—*A. ararauna* has a tiny space between the base of the beak and the start of its plumage. The Blue and Gold Macaw has a bare region from the base of the lower mandible up to the lower cheek area: this region is fully feathered—a blue-green color." The facial skin of the Blue-throated Macaw is generally flesh-colored to red, the Blue and Gold is normally white here, although in some cases red.

Dissemination: Bolivia, Paraguay and Northern Argentina. There the handsome Blue-throated Macaw inhabits the extension of the East-Cordillion, in warm swamp areas and gallery forests. It can sometimes be found in swarms with the Blue and Gold Macaw and the Scarlet Macaw, but in fewer numbers than either of these species. Lantermann regards the Blue-throated Macaw as a near relation of the Blue and Gold: "The geography of the two animals indicates the congruent dissemination of closely related species, without any recognizable crosses within the species or as a sub-species." And finally, research by Reinhard, 1982 completely verifies that the two species are distinct, based on differing vocal patterns.

Status: Not much is known of this species' breeding. It probably lasts from December to April.

This bird was considered until recently a "fabled bird," it was not kept by Europeans in earlier times—or it was simply unknown. There is only one known skin, being held in the British Museum in London. Hoppe estimates 15 to 20 presently being kept in Germany, between zoological gardens and bird enthusiasts. In 1979-1980 a few Blue-throated Macaws came from South America through the European bird market and were sold for more than $5,000 US dollars apiece. The Walsrode Bird Park has a pair, and the Berlin Zoo is in possession of an endoscopic pair. R. Burkard, of Switzerland has four birds of this species on the grounds of his home, and Kiessling has a couple in Teneriffa. In contrast with the comfort loving *A. ararauna*, *A. glaucogularis* is quite

lively and apparently more intelligent. Hoppe mentions four birds on display in the Walsrode Park, one of which is suspected of plucking at the feathers of the other three birds.

Hayward (1983) describes the successful breeding of the Blue-throated Macaw by the South African breeder Gill du Venage, Transvaal. In total four birds were raised.

De Grahl authors a detailed report which I've reprinted because of its sensational beginning:

"The Parrot Zoo in Puerte de la Cruz on Teneriffa received in 1980 and 1981 a pair of endoscopic birds, whose sexes were barely distinguishable. This pair lives in a aviary 5.1 m (16.7 ft) long, 3.6 m (12 ft) wide and 4.2 m (13.7 ft) high. Only the front and roof are made of fencing, the other sides are solid, to give the birds privacy, and protection from the wind. The nest is 80 cm (31.5 in) high, with a floor measuring 50 x 60 cm (20 x 24 in); the entrance is 12 cm (5 in) in diameter. This nest is attached quite high on a wall. The floor has about 10 cm (4 in) of sawdust. Pine branches are attached to the rather large climbing stand each week, which are eagerly plucked off by the macaws."

"The nest originally served as a roost, but in July 1984, the female spent more time during the day inside the nest. The first egg was seen on the 10th of July. It measured 44 x 34 mm (1.7 x 1.3 in); the second measured 42 x 32 mm (1.6 x 1.2 in)."

"Both eggs were fertilized, but the second egg died as an embryo. After approximately 26-27 days, on the 5th and 6th of August, a small macaw hatched. Both parents took care of the young bird. To begin with, the feed consisted of various fruits, vegetables, chopped chicken eggs, soaked white bread with vitamins and minerals added; also sprouted seeds."

"It is delightful that new knowledge of a relatively unknown bird can be obtained through handling in an aviary. By my observations, the Blue-throated Macaw seems to be a quiet bird, its cry rarely heard. Immature Blue-throated Macaws appear to have a whitish cere, while the older birds have flesh-colored ceres. By the beginning of January, the immature was recognizable by its bright irises, and its darker cheeks. It had reached the size of its parents."

Baby Catalina. Macaws require an abundance of their owner's time. A careful consideration as to the amount of time one will actually be able to spend with the bird should be accounted for prior to the purchase.

RED-FRONTED MACAW

Scientific Name: *Ara rubrogenys*, Lafresnaye, 1847

Common Names: Red-fronted Macaw, Red-cheeked Macaw, Lafresnaye's Macaw.

Field Marks: 60 cm (23.6 in) long; olive green general plumage; yellowish overtone to the head and neck; red panels on the feathers of the forehead, ear coverts, and thighs; many birds have red specks on the outermost parts of the breast and abdomen feathers; wing edge, carpal edge, and shoulder coverts orange-red; larger under wing coverts and under side of the tail olive-yellow; gray-blue tips on the flight feathers and primary coverts; inner web of the primaries, overlaid with black; under side of the wing and top side of the tail olive-green with blue throughout; cheek skins rose, with dark, almost black feather strips; thin bare stripes between the base of the beak and the eyes; beak black; toes black/brown; irises orange. The females are probably smaller in body size and beak, and have less plumage in the facial region.

Dissemination: Bolivia: Chochabamba and Santa

Red-Fronted Macaw, *Ara rubrogenys*. The Red-Fronted Macaw proves to be very beautiful yet unusual in color. Predominantly green in color with orange-red on the forehead, cheeks, and bend in the wing. The wing coverts and thighs are orange. The primary feathers are blue.

Cruz provinces.

Range: Fifteen years ago, this species was thought to be extinct; only prepared skins could be found in museums. Old sources indicated that the species lived in the Nebel forests of Yungas, and in the fruitful highlands of the eastern slopes in the Chochabamba province in Central Bolivia. Hoppe described the habitat: "This rare species lives at an altitude of 1300-2000 m (4200-6500 ft.) above sea level, in an area characterized by arid forests and cactus during the rainy season, otherwise dry rivers and brooks swell in their course to the Gran Chaco river." Outside of the

Red-fronted Macaw, *Ara rubrogenys*. Red-fronted macaws especially like to eat citrus fruits. Too much is not good to feed your bird. As with humans, moderation is the key.

breeding season, this handsome bird roams its habitat nomadically in swarms of about 80 birds, searching for nourishment in the form of shrubs, and tree fruits such as cactus seeds. The Red-fronted Macaw will frequently search the ground for food, which rarely occurs among the other macaw species. This bird is unpopular among the neighboring Indians because of the considerable damage they do to the peanut and corn crops. The natives also hunt the bird for its flesh and feathers.

In Cordier's correspondence with De Grahl, this macaw species is said to be found also in

hot, dry areas; it is most frequently observed at altitudes above 2000 m (6500 ft).

No research is available on this bird's nest building, breeding, or raising of its young in the wild. The natives believe that this bird nests in branches that it has placed in the crevices of cliffs; this has not yet been documented.

Status: The English woman R. Low reports (1980) that the first bird of this species was imported into England in the beginning of 1970. J. Halford, of Hampshire, and R. Burkhard of Switzerland are known to keep these birds, most likely procuring them from the expert trapper Cordier. Unfortunately Burkhard's female has a broken wing. A bit later the Red-fronted Macaw was seen in Walsrode and the Zoological Gardens of Berlin and Wuppertal. At first it was quite difficult to feed these birds: they would only eat cracked cornfeed. The birds seem to adapt well to the often cold climate of central Europe. The first bird was sold in the United States for an enormous sum in 1976 according to Decoteau (1982). In 1977, 16 more were brought in, in 1978, 82, and in 1979, 125 birds were imported, so that a significant portion of the free-living population, estimated at 3,000, was irresponsibly destroyed. German trade journals have been advertising large numbers of these birds for sale. Hoppe came into possession of a bird of this species, but found it had a serious problem: at first it would eat only sunflower seeds, and would vomit if disturbed. It finally began eating corn, but never became tame—in fact it kept more and more distance between itself and its keeper. The bird was finally given up to a breeder in Switzerland.

Hoppe gives details of the mating dance: "The mating dance of the Red-fronted Macaw is a fascinating spectacle. The male hangs his wings, fully showing the orange-red edge. He strolls back and forth along the branch (stand), emitting shrill whistles. His pupils dilate, making the bright orange irises even more prominent. His dance can last 10-15 minutes, and ends with him feeding his mate and finally the two birds copulate."

Because the Red-fronted Macaw is under species protection, attempts are being made to establish colonies in some zoological gardens.

Although *Avicultural Magazine* 1983, cites the first successful breeding of a captive Red-fronted Macaw as having happened in the Jersey Wildlife Preservation Trust, the Wuppertal Zoo kept a pair which produced three young birds in 1978, which were hand-fed shortly after hatching. The next year the pair fully raised two young birds themselves. By 1981, the Wuppertal Zoo boasted of

Red-fronted Macaws, *Ara rubrogenys*. The Red-fronted macaw is considered to be a threatened species. Its only chance at survival is captive breeding.

having raised six of these birds there—keeping a total of ten birds. One of the birds was moved to the Wilhalmina Zoo in Stuttgart. It still had not begun to display the red coloration on its head. The most recent was announced by the March, 1985 issue of *The Feathered World* : three young Red-fronted Macaws were raised in the East Berlin Zoo.

Apparently the Red-fronted Macaw, equally happy in private hands or in small breeding groups, prefers nests hung horizontally, as are found in the Wuppertal Zoo.

CHESTNUT-FRONTED MACAW

Scientific Name:*Ara severa*, Linne, 1758

Common Name: Severe Macaw

Field Marks: There are two sub-species distinguished under the species *Ara severa.* The nominal form, *Ara severa severa* (Linne): 46 cm (18 in) long; green; reddish-brown forehead, chin and cheek border; bluish-green front and top of head; cream-colored cheek skin, almost entirely unfeathered, with numerous black stripes of feathers; outer web of primaries and primary

coverts blue; wing edge, carpal edge, and under wing coverts scarlet-red; reddish-brown underside of wings; lower thigh plumage red; large under wing coverts olive-green; topside of tail feathers reddish-brown, blue-green towards the end, underside of the tail dark orange-red; under wing coverts orange; beak dark-gray; feet gray; irises reddish-brown.

The female has a somewhat thinner reddish-brown foreheadband (in their first year they have no band around the forehead,

and are smaller in size); the immatures have brownish irises.

The second sub-species, *A. severa castaneifrons* (Lafresnaye), resembles the nominal form in color, but is larger in size.

Dissemination: *A. severa severa*: Central Northern Venezuela, French Guyana, south to northwestern Mato Grosso, northern Goias, and northwestern Bahia, in Brazil. *A. severa castaneifrons*: eastern Panama, western Colombia, Venezuela, eastern Peru, northern Bolivia, northwestern Brazil.

Range: In its homeland, the Chestnut-fronted Macaw is still frequently seen, at least in some areas. It typically inhabits the tropical regions, where it prefers the forested river basins, but can also be found searching for food in agricultural districts (corn and grains). It feeds principally on wild fruits, berries, and seeds. Figs, mangos, and the seed of the euphorbio plant seem to be its favorite foods.

Red-fronted Macaw, *Ara rubrogenys*. Macaws do best when housed in a large aviary that has many planted trees within it.

Severe Macaw, *Ara severa.*
The Severe Macaw quickly becomes confiding to its owner and becomes very tame. They also prove to be very gifted talkers.

The birds leave their roosts early in the morning in small groups of 5 to 20 birds. Research by P. Roth (1982), indicates that the *A. severa* competes with the *A. ararauna, A. chloroptera, A. macao,* and *A. manilata* in its search for nourishment. Considerable damage is done by this bird in the fruit plantations, and it is often hunted with shotguns. The return to the roost takes place in the late afternoon, where as many as a hundred birds can be seen as they loudly search for that night's perch.

A. severa has been known to socialize with Blue-headed Pionus; specifically in S.W. Panama this phenomenon has been observed.

The breeding periods differ by region: In northern Colombia the bird breeds in January/February, in Panama in February/ March. They nest in empty woodpecker holes, or in widened openings in dead palm trees.

In the southernmost regions, the birds breed as early as November, three to five eggs measuring 38 x 30 mm (1.5 x 1.1) are clutched from 26-28 days. The young birds leave their nest some 70 days after hatching.

Interesting observations on their natural breeding habits were made by P. Roth (his personal commentary, quoted by Hoppe, 1983): "The breeding season lasts from about the beginning of November to the end of January. In January: in a tree 30 m (99 ft.) high, *A. severa* put a hole 23 m (76 ft.) up, in a dead side branch into use, presumably raising its young there. In November of the same year (1978), two Chestnut-fronted Macaws moved into a hole 28 m (92 ft) high in a Brazil nut tree. At this height the trunk still had a diameter of over 250 cm (99 in.). On the 24th of December, the tree was climbed and the nest inspected. Two young birds and a damaged egg were found. The oldest immature was about three weeks old, the other four to six days younger.

"This same tree was found to have tree termites. Some time earlier the termite hole had been used as a nest by two to four pairs of Golden-winged Parakeets. A short time later a pair of White-eyed Conures built a nest about 1.2 m (4 ft) lower than the macaw nest."

Status: Parrot enthusiasts who have had experience with the Chestnut-fronted Macaw unanimously praise the ease with which this bird is tamed and its exceptional imitative abilities. Hoppe even had a bird who could speak a few words in Spanish. With regard to their tropical origins, newly imported birds need a constant room temperature of about 20°C (68°F). It is said that the French naturalist Buffon considered the Chestnut-fronted Macaw an intelligent and diligent pupil.

De Grahl writes that the first captive birds were bred in 1940 in the San Diego Zoo. Breeding may already have been achieved for twenty years: K. Neunzig (1921) writes of a pair belonging to a breeder named Sharland, who lost the first brood to a thunderstorm, and produced a second, of which nothing is known.

O. Hirthe, Copenhagen, 1954, produced the first European born *A. severa*. After two full months, one immature emerged from the nest, and was fed by its parents for another six weeks. Four years later the same pair produced four young birds out of five eggs. The Whipsnade Zoo of London had some success with this species in 1961. In 1963 H. Kleiser repeated the experience, in Hof Zoo. On several occasions, his pair laid three eggs, which were brooded for 24 days. De Grahl speculates that H. Kleiser was breeding *A. nobilis* rather than *A. severa* (a yellower upper mandible, and brighter irises). P. Mullick in India produced a brood in 1968, as did the Cincinnatti Zoo in 1970.

K. Oehler, of Friedrickshafen, succeeded in mating a Chestnut-fronted Macaw with Illiger's Macaw (*A. maracana*). Hoppe dates this in 1964.

YELLOW-COLLARED MACAW

Scientific Name: *Ara auricollis*, Cassin, 1853

Common Names: Yellow-collared Macaw, Golden-naped Macaw, Cassin's Macaw.

Field Marks: 38-39 cm (15-15.5 in) long; dark

green; forehead, top of head, and cheeks brownish-black with green overlay; back of the head green-blue; yellow band around neck; cheeks yellow-white, entirely nude; primaries blue; outer webs of the outermost secondaries blue; underside of the wing green; underside of the tail blue with brownish tips; underside of the wings yellow to olive-green; beak black with lighter tip; feet flesh-colored; irises brownish-red.

The neck band should be thinner on the female bird. Immatures are a brighter green with a less noticeable neck band, and have a few yellow specks on their breast plumage.

Although Decoteau (1982) writes of two varieties, distinguished by either yellow or a more orange-colored neck band, no separate sub-species have been established.

Dissemination: Brazil, Mato Grosso, Bolivia, Paraguay, northwestern Argentina.

Range: This species is found in a variety of habitats. The Yellow-collared Macaw is found in the highlands, as well as the swamps and river basins: thorn bush savannas, and arid regions of Bolivia, as well as the virgin forests along the Rio Mamore, Rio Blanco, and Itenez or Guapore rivers, in which the birds find nourishment, shelter, and freedom to breed. In the vast swamps of the Paraguay lowlands, there are more specimens than in the dry, hot Chaco area of western Paraguay.

Out of breeding season, swarms have been counted numbering up to 500 birds

(Gomex, Goodfellow). This species seems to be quite gregarious, although quarreling constantly with many shrieks over the best sitting spots seems to be a daily occupation. Especially in the roost, the lively yelling prevails well into the darkness. Early in the morning the birds leave their roost in search of food. Most likely they feed on figs, and principally the fruit of various palm trees, besides leaf and flower buds.

Pairing indicates the beginning of the breeding season; in the southernmost areas of dissemination, the courting dance happens shortly after the rainy season sets in. Most clutches consist of three eggs, laid in the beginning of December, at intervals of two days. Breeding season starts somewhat later in the northern reaches of this bird's habitat; but in January, most clutches are complete. Whether or not the male participates in the brooding of the eggs has not been confirmed by observation, but Hoppe supposes that indeed he does. Brooding lasts 27-28 days, with the young remaining in the nest for another 10-11 weeks.

Status: In the beginning of 1970 the Yellow-collared Macaw was seldom kept in Europe, either as caged or aviary birds. Only a few zoos were able to obtain this bird. After 1973 it had become relatively common, and was successfully bred in private aviaries. In recent years only a few isolated birds have reached Germany. They become tame astonishingly fast, and even when kept in groups will delicately perch on a hand.

Hoppe graphically depicts his own experiences: "One bird, being kept in an aviary, was so tame after just one week that he let himself be touched. His greatest amusement was to be laid on his back while his belly was scratched. His tameness almost became a burden: it became almost impossible to get him off your shoulder. He seemed to be generally more reserved with women; only when there were no men within his reach would he allow himself to be picked up by a woman. He was entirely unskilled in learning to imitate noises, whistles, or words; he did not have any recognizable speaking ability."

In contrast there have been a few Yellow-collared Macaws known to have been not only very playful, but learned numerous

Opposite: Yellow - collared Macaw, *Ara auricollis.* The Yellow - collared macaw tends to be very aggressive towards other birds and should not be housed with any other parrots except its own kind.

words and melodies.

These birds have also been kept in partial freedom. Living in the vicinity of pine forests, the birds were let out of their aviaries in the summer months, to spend the day among the pines, where they enjoyed picking the seed out of the pinecones. In the evening, they always returned back home to feed.

The loud calls of this species can be quite unpleasant. They are especially noisy at dawn, but very often scream for no apparent reason. It is recommended that a person wishing to keep a bird of this species, first speak of it to the neighbors. It is sometimes possible to quiet the birds by darkening their quarters. Caution must also be taken against this species' aggression towards other birds, although it is certainly possible to keep the birds in pairs.

The Walsrode Bird Zoo can take credit for the first German breeding in 1976, although the facts indicate that the first captive breeding took place at Busch Gardens, in Tampa, FL, in 1968.

One bird was raised in Walsrode, in 1976; since that time 27 young Yellow-collared Macaws have been brought up in that Zoo. Evidence supporting the noteworthy breeding by K. Maass, in Drensteinfurt as the first German captive breeding, as Hoppe suggests, is unclear. The International Zoo Yearbook of 1977 gives the Walsrode breeding as 1976. In August of 1978, Maass did mate a pair of birds acquired in 1976, only the young disappeared a short time after hatching.

Again in 1979 the pair, in an isolated aviary (with a nest measuring 70 cm (28 in.) high and 35 cm (14 in.) in diameter, laid another three eggs. The nest was sprayed with a liter of water each day. At the end of June the eggs hatched. Their pleas for food were audible and easily recognizable. The parents would not allow the nest to be inspected. Within 11 weeks the young macaws left their nest.

This same pair mated successfully again the next year. Their young fledglings had yellow feathers sprinkled among their breast plumage, their general plumage was a brighter green, and the yellow neck band was less pronounced than those of their parents. Besides the usual parrot feed, the breeder fed the birds the following, in paste form: an egg, with two tablespoons of honeycomb, one tablespoon of bread flour, one tablespoon cooked rice, two tablespoons cooked corn, one-half teaspoon dextrose, one and one-half teaspoon carrot custard with egg yolk and two middle-sized smashed carrots.

In 1978 a young Yellow-collared Macaw hatched in an aviary in Switzerland, and the Zoological Garden in Bristol achieved the first brood in England.

H. Ploog, of Seedorf, Germany, bred a pair of birds that he had segregated from a small group of four birds. The

Yellow-collared Macaw, *Ara auricollis.* As a pet, the yellow-collared macaw is quite adapted and pleasant to have around. They tame fairly easily and can also be taught to speak with little effort.

nest was 100 cm (39 in.) high, and 30 cm (12 in.) in diameter. Out of three fertilized eggs, three chicks hatched in the beginning of June, 1981. The parents raised the chicks without any problems, and 69 days after they were born, the oldest left the nest. The fledged bird returned each night to the nest, and was fed by its parents for yet another month. While they were raising the young birds, the parent birds fed exclusively on sprouted sunflower seeds, and a dry parrot mixture.

BLUE-HEADED MACAW

Scientific Name: *Ara couloni*, Sclater, 1876

Common Name: Blue-headed Macaw, Coulon's Macaw

Field Marks: 41 cm (16 in) long; general plumage green; forehead and cheeks blue; turquoise back of the head; underside olive-green to yellowish; primaries, outermost secondaries, as well as outermost large wing coverts all blue; wing edging blue; topside of tail feathers reddish-brown with blue tips; underside of tail yellow-green; the small bare cheek skin and eyering white to gray; beak black with brighter ridge, and grayer tip; feet dark gray (Lantermann), flesh-colored (Hoppe); irises

yellow. Sexual distinctions in plumage, etc. and immature markings are unknown.

Dissemination: Peru (Central part: the province of Loreto), probably also in the outermost western regions of the Brazilian provinces of Amazonas, and Acre.

Range: According to the current state of research (Taylor, 1958), it is believed that *A. couloni* is not a sub-species of *A. maracana*, as was once believed, and although closely related, it is a separate species. O'Neill ascertained this research in 1969 by verifying that the Blue-headed Macaw has a softer and higher pitched cry. Further studies have only substantiated this position. The species was named by P.L. Sclater, in 1876, who received a prepared skin from De Coulon, and named it after him.

Forshaw reports the observations made by O'Neill in Brazil (1973). Pairs and groups of these birds were recognized along the Curanja River in Balta at heights of up to 300 meters (984 ft). According to Hoppe, this extremely rare bird lives primarily in the Montana Mountain region: the unexplored virgin forests in the eastern part of the East-Cordillion in Peru. To the north its habitat is limited by the Huallaga and Maranon Rivers. The westernmost region of their range is the east extension of the East-Cordillion in the Apurimac and Ucayali Valleys; in the south, the Cordillera de Dios, and in the East, the Brazilian border.

The habitat of the Blue-headed Macaw is only a small speck in the geography of South America. But oppressive heat in the dry season, high humidity, and huge areas, nearly unpopulated, make this district quite inaccessible to ornithological research. It is unknown whether the Blue-headed Macaw breeds during the rainy season in the months of October to April; it is most likely that they do.

Status: In 1913, the Berlin Zoo kept a bird of this species, from which a published photograph still exists that has proved useful upon more than one occasion. D. West, of the United States had a male bird in 1959. To this day, however, parrot specialists, armed with the best of parrot equipment from the Walsrode and San Diego Zoos, have not been able to successfully keep a bird of this species in captivity. I have been able to find no records of this ornithological rarity being kept captively in its homeland.

A specimen was obtained on the 18th of November, 1961, along Rip Pachitea (a tributary of the Ucayali) in Hacienda Flor by Puerto Victoria, in rain forests laying at 350 m (1150 ft) altitude. This skin can be found among the collection of the Senckenberg Museum, in Frankfurt am Main. It was a male, weighing 267g (8.6 oz), and measuring 39.5 cm (16 in.) long. The wings are 24 cm (10 in.) long. According to Decoteau (1982) there are presently four Blue-headed Macaws living in the U.S.A., among which is a pair of sexually mature birds. There are no known birds of this species living either as caged or aviary birds in Europe.

RED-BELLIED MACAW

Scientific Name: *Ara manilata*, Boddaert, 1783

Field Marks: 49 cm (19 in.) long; dark green; chin, throat and upper breast greenish-gray, bordered with yellow-green; belly and rump plumage brownish-red; thighs blue-green with brighter edging; thigh plumage green with reddish edging; underside and sides of the neck are otherwise olive-green;

Pair of Red-Bellied Macaws, *Ara manilata.* The Red-bellied macaw is the largest of the small macaws and the dullest in color.

forehead and crown green-blue; primaries dark blue, with blue-black edging on the inner webs, outer webs of the outermost large wing coverts greenish-blue; underside of the wings yellow-green; under wing coverts yellow-green; upper tail coverts green with yellow edging; under tail coverts blue-green; top side of the tail green; underside of the tail yellow-green; cheek region unfeathered, yellowish; bill gray-black; toes dark gray; irises dark brown.

There is no known difference either in size or coloring between the two sexes. Immatures have dark brown specks on their bellies, and are somewhat smaller; the plumage of the immatures may also be black or brownish on the head (Low, 1980).

Range: The island of Trinidad, Guyana, north and southeastern Venezuela, Colombia, northern Peru, the Mato Grosso province of Brazil; and according to Hoppe, also in northern Goias and western Bahia.

Habitat: The Red-bellied Macaw is thought to be quite common in its natural habitat. Nonetheless, very little is known of its feeding, social behavior, or breeding. Hoppe repeatedly identified the species in Trinidad and Guyana. Another researcher spotted a swarm with over 100 individuals. Herklots observed the Red-bellied Macaw in the company of the Orange-winged Amazon. He also writes that this species has increased in numbers on the island of Trinidad. This optimistic view must be approached skeptically. Industrialization and the development of the oil industry are more commonly

believed to have encroached on the existence of these birds.

The fruit of the Mauritia Palm (*Mauritia flexuosa*), which the birds seek in the morning hours, is their preferred food. They let out shrill cries as they fly, quieting when they reach their feeding trees. Their days are spent sleeping and preening, enjoying a bath when it happens to rain. They return to their roosts late in the afternoon. They are protected from predators by roosting in trees on islands in rivers and swamps.

In the southernmost range, the breeding season begins in the beginning of January. The female lays an average of two eggs per clutch in holes of dead palm trees. The length of the clutching period and time the chicks stay in the nest after hatching are unknown. After the breeding season, the parents and their new young rejoin the flock.

Status: There have been few of these birds kept either in cages or in aviaries of the world. According to Decoteau (1982), there are pairs living in the United States, and an isolated pair is known to live in England. Hoppe was verbally informed by Silve that an American breeder by the name of G. Harrison of Florida, has successfully bred a pair of Red-bellied Macaws.

The Walsrode Bird park managed to import a bird of this rarely seen species in 1973; further information regarding importation of this bird is unclear. The Englishman J. Halford from Hampshire writes of the uncommon insatiable need his bird seems to have for warmth: it stays in the heated inner chamber of its aviary year 'round (Low, 1980). Hoppe

Red-bellied macaw, *Ara manilata*. Although not as vividly colored as the other macaws, the red-bellied is still a playful, affectionate, and intelligent pet.

corroborates this, saying that the animal handlers from the birds' habitats find this species to be susceptible to low temperatures. Kept at temperatures lower than 20°C (68°F), they become cold, so the author recommends that the birds be kept in a heated chamber with a daytime temperature of at least 25°C (77°F), and a nighttime temperature no lower than 20°C (68°F). A relative humidity of 80%, as is found in the birds' natural habitat is also advised.

The feed should be carefully varied. Decoteau and Lantermann agree that the birds prefer apples, pears, bananas, oranges, and papayas to the parrot feed. Nuts also belong with the mentioned foods.

MILITARY MACAW

Scientific Name: *Ara militaris*, Linne, 1766

The Military Macaw is divided into three sub-species:

(1) *Ara militaris militaris* (Linne); called the Military Macaw.

Field Marks: 70 cm (28 in) long; olive green, more pronounced on the rump and wings; lower back and upper tail coverts blue; primaries and secondaries blue; wing underside greenish-yellow; rump plumage clear blue; upperside of tail brownish-red; tail feathers brownish-red with blue tips; tail and wing undersides yellow-olive; head feathers a somewhat clearer green color than that of the general plumage; blue shimmer to the hind part of head or skull; throat brownish; forehead and lore strips bright red; blackish-green feather stripes run along the otherwise reddish cheek region; bill gray-black; feet blackish-brown; irises yellow. The female of this species has a slightly smaller head. Immatures have more brownish irises.

Range: Northwestern Venezuela, Colombia, north-eastern Ecuador, Peru, in the provinces of Lambayeque and Cajamarca.

(2) *Ara militaris mexicana* (Ridgeway); known as the Mexican Military Macaw.

Field Marks: same as the nominal form, but this bird is noticeably larger.

Range: Central Mexico from the southeastern area of Sonora and the southwestern region of Chihuahua down through the isthmus of Tehuantepec; South Nuevo Leon and southern Tamaulipas southward through the province of Mexico.

(3) *Ara militaris boliviana* (Reichenow), Bolivian Military Macaw.

Field Marks: Somewhat larger than *A. m. militaris*; its throat specks more of a reddish-brown; ear coverts have redder bases; the primaries and tips of the tails have a more intense blue.

Range: Southeastern Bolivia, and Argentina (Eastern Jujuy and Northern Salta).

A fourth sub-species was designated by A. J. von Rossem and M. Hachisuka in 1939; *Ara militaris sheffleri* was never documented scientifically. A specimen of the animal was never obtained to verify the zoological nomenclature, as is customary. Hoppe considers it questionable "whether this bird was an actual form of either of the Military Macaws."

Range: The Military Macaw has been observed in altitudes of up to 2500 m (8200 ft), on the deciduous mountain slopes; in arid regions and occasionally among the mountain valleys. The bird probably ventures sometimes into the deeper lying tracts of land in its search for food. They are rarely seen in the tropical rain forests, which is the typical habitat for the Scarlet Macaw.

Numerous vitamin- and mineral-fortified foods exist on the market. Some, such as the one shown, can even be served warm. Photo courtesy of Pretty Bird International.

The geographical race *A. m. militaris* is occasionally seen in Northern Peru on the slopes of Maranon, in the Central Cordillion. The bird is thought to seek the steep Pacific cliffs in the months of September and October. The habitat of *A. m. mexicana* frequently has frost and snowfall. Hoppe wrote of his trip through Mexico and mentions a single Military Macaw that he saw sitting in a fig tree. "It was presumably a male bird, sitting near its nest keeping watch, while his mate sat upon the eggs" (1983).

The breeding season occurs at different times depending on the region: generally in the months of March and April, and May or June in the dry months. The birds pair off only in this time of the year, otherwise living in groups of 10 to 30 birds. They feed on seeds, buds and berries, but also fruits, especially figs.

The pair moves into their brooding nests at this time, in areas to which they return yearly, generally using the abandoned holes of woodpeckers. The subspecies *A. militaris boliviana* breeds in the months of November and December. The nest of a Military Macaw was found in a fallen tree; it had a inner diameter of 33 cm (13 in), and had stood 20 m (66 ft) over the ground. The floor of the nest was laid with rough wood chips. The clutch usually consists of three eggs, and lasts 25 to 26 days. The chicks are raised for about three months.

Although the Military Macaws are more commonly seen in captivity than their larger cousin *A. ambigua*, they also belong to the category of seldom imported Macaw species. Most individuals of this species should be fairly able imitators. There have also been instances of artistic performances by carefully trained birds. Since this species does not seem to be especially sensitive, they can be kept in West Germany on open grounds in the summer, without special heating arrangements. In the wintertime, the Military Macaw certainly needs the protection of a heated room, unless the temperatures stay within a tropical range.

Captive breedings of this species have occurred infrequently, although there have been reports of mix-ups with the Buffon's Macaw. Breeders have found their unusually loud cries a problem. One would do well to make suitable arrangements with the neighbors.

Successful breedings: Wellington Zoo, New Zealand, 1973 (Hoppe): according to Lantermann pairs were mated there in as early as 1963; Fort Worth Zoo, 1964; East Berlin Zoo 1974 and 1975; Busch Gardens, in Tampa, 1978; and by P.V. Springman, TX, 1978. In the United States, there have been other couplings, but none of these have been scientifically documented (Decoteau, 1982).

There are usually two, and upon exception three eggs laid (measuring 46 x 33 mm/2 x 1.5 in.), which are clutched for 27 days. After 11 to 14 weeks, the fully feathered birds leave their nests. Hybrids have probably been bred ever since 1901: female Military Macaw with a male Scarlet Macaw, in the London Zoo. Eggs have also been produced from a mating of a male Military Macaw and female Scarlet Macaws, and female Green-winged Macaws.

BUFFON'S MACAW

Scientific Name: *Ara ambigua*, Bechstein, 1811.

There are two sub-species:

(1) *Ara ambigua ambigua* (Bechstein), called Buffon's Macaw or the Grand Military Macaw.

Field Marks: 85 cm (33 in.)long; olive-green, somewhat brighter than *A. militaris*, with yellowish suffusion; primaries and secondaries blue; large wing coverts edged with blue; underside of wing clear olive-green; lower back and tips of the upper tail coverts clear blue; upper tail coverts brownish-red; underside of tail bright olive-green with darker edging; almost completely nude facial skin with narrow black lines of

Opposite: Military Macaw, *Ara militaris*, with Barrel Nest. The nest box for a macaw must be constructed in such a way that it is very difficult to destroy. Most, such as the one pictured here, have a sheet metal covering over any areas that would be beginning demolition sites.

feathers; bill dark gray with bright tip; gray feet; yellowish irises. Head and beak are a bit smaller on the female birds. The immatures are recognizable by their brownish irises.

Range: Nicaragua, Costa Rica, Panama, western Colombia.

The sub-species *Ara ambigua guayaquilensis* (Chapman) is also known as Buffon's Macaw, Ecuadorian Macaw, or Chapman's Green Macaw.

Field Marks: Almost identical to the *A. a. ambigua*, however with green undersides of the wings and tail, also has a bit smaller bill.

Range: Western Ecuador, probably also in southwestern Colombia. The two sub-species have distinct ranges.

Habitat: With respect to the works of some ornithologists, it is not definite whether Buffon's Macaw and the Military Macaw are distinct species. Hoppe regards it probable that *A. ambigua* is in fact a separate species. He offers the following explanation: "The *Ara ambigua* typically lives at altitudes up to 800 m (2600 ft.). On the other hand *A. militaris* is rarely seen at altitudes lower than 600 m (2000 ft.), and then only in quick searches for food. It is thought to stay in the range of 600 to 2500 m (2000 to 8000 ft). If one deviates from this, and identifies the *A. ambigua*, and the *A. militaris* as one species, one must also establish a connecting range, reaching from Central Mexico to Ecuador" (1983).

Buffon's Macaw are typically found in tropical virgin forests, which they inhabit along with the Scarlet Macaw (in N.E. Nicaragua, and Costa Rica). In recent years 50% of existing birds are estimated as having been lost to the clearing of forests for agriculture and lumber removal. The moist and arid savannas no longer offer this macaw species the necessary support; for this reason, Buffon's Macaw is probably already extinct in Honduras.

Their numbers are still relatively large in the sparsely populated Caribbean coastal area east of the Cordillera Central and Cordillera de Talamanca. Sporadic occurrences also are found on the Pacific coast of Costa Rica.

According to R. S. Ridgely (1981), this species has been extinct in the Canal Zone for a number of years now. East of the Panama Canal to the border of Colombia, in the lowlands of Darien, one still can find this bird. This area has plenty of tropical forests, savannas, and mangrove swamps for the bird to feed on, and wooded area for protection of roosting and breeding. Central to the range of this species is the delta of the Atrato River with its extensive swamps. In this hot, humid climate, Buffon's Macaw feels at home.

The sub-species *A. ambigua guayaquilensis* inhabits a relatively small region, distinct from the nominal form, from S.W. Colombia to the Gulf of Guayaquil, in Ecuador. This area also yields rich coastal tropics, mangrove swamps, and humid savannas.

Open areas are avoided by both sub-species entirely, although they certainly will fly over such areas in their search for food. Unlike most other macaw species, Buffon's Macaw does not seek out the society of large swarms, preferring to live in pairs, or family groups. Many ornithologists have spotted the birds, however, in groups of up to 12 birds. They feed on various seeds, fruits, berries, nuts, buds, and greens.

The flight of this species is described as quick and rapacious. When invaded in the treetops, they let out their especially loud shrieks, and spend their time eating, preening, and napping.

They begin to breed with the onset of the rainy season, varying according to region in December and January. Although no verified research has been con-ducted, it is agreed that the female clutches two or

Military Macaw, *Ara militaris*, & Buffon's Macaw, *Ara ambigua*. The Buffon's Macaw is similar to the Military except for the green of the general plumage is paler and more yellowish and the forehead is scarlet red in color rather than red.

three eggs, measuring 55 x 46 mm (2.2 x 1.8 in), alone. The immatures probably remain in the nest for about 100 days.

Status: Buffon's Macaw has always been rare in captivity. The Berlin Zoo kept the first in 1898. Since then, they have been valued for their aptitude in imitation, easy taming, and agility. Unfortunately many of these birds are kept as solitary pets, and not given the opportunity to reproduce, although there are even fewer Buffon's Macaws in captivity than the Hyacinth Macaw.

It is hoped that by and by individual birds will be brought into the company of at least one other bird. Matings are expected in the following Zoos: East Berlin, Bochum, Walsrode, and Cornwall. This rare bird was successfully mated in the East Berlin Zoo in 1974. Both the United States and England are thought to have mating birds, but none as yet have been confirmed. Since English trade journals in the past have not made the distinction between *A. ambigua* and *A. militaris*, some of the matings found therein may have been of the *A. ambigua*.

There was a Buffon's Macaw hand-raised in Bird Paradise, in Cornwall, England (M. Reynolds). Afterwards the pair of macaws was kept in an open flight. Given the risk of escape, some of the flight feathers were clipped, confining the flight of the birds. The first clutch, in April, 1976, ended in broken eggs. The first young birds hatched in the following year. One egg was placed under a Yellow-collared Macaw (*Ara auricollis*), who had been bred to a Scarlet Macaw. The second egg was placed in an incubator; the third in the nest of a pair of free-flying Scarlet Macaws.

The hybrid pair brooded one chick and the young Buffon's Macaw, which died after three days. The egg in the incubator also died. Only the third chick, brooded by the pair of Scarlet Macaws, survived. It was recognizable as a Military Macaw within one month. When it was ten weeks old, the young macaw was hand-fed, to further ascertain its survival. After another three weeks, the immature had reached independence.

Decoteau reported in 1982 of a successful breeding by a species whose name was unrecognizable.

The Wilhelmina Zoo in Stuttgart has repeatedly produced chicks from a male Buffon's Macaw and a female Scarlet Macaw. A few have been further bred, producing beautifully feathered birds with lively natures in their large open aviaries. Further breeding will be possible if owners of Buffon's Macaw bring their animals together with birds of the opposite sex. It is also questionable whether or not the keeping of these birds in parrot collections, chained to their climbing frames, is an ethical practice.

In addition: On the occasion of the 5th conference from the 22nd of April to the 3rd of May, 1985 in Buenos Aires, the Buffon's Macaw was transferred from Appendum II to Appendum I of the Washington Endangered Species list.

GREEN-WINGED MACAW

Scientific Name: *Ara chloroptera*, G. R. Gray, 1859

Common Names: Green-winged Macaw, Red and Green Macaw

Field Marks: 90 cm (36 in.)long; dark red general plumage; middle wing coverts, inner secondaries and shoulder feathers green; large wing coverts on the outer webs and primaries and secondaries blue; outer webs of the primaries dark blue; rump, upper and under tail coverts bright blue; tail dark red with blue tips; outermost tail feathers blue on the outerwebs; undersides of tail and wings dark red; cheek region has thin reddish feather stripes; the facial skin is otherwise nude, white; upper mandible horn colored; dark gray base of the side of the bill; lower mandible gray-black; feet dark grayish-brown; irises yellow. Females of this species are smaller in body size and in the length of their feathers. Immatures have brownish irises, and their tail feathers are shorter. The base of their upper mandible is a clearer gray than those of its parents.

Range: Eastern Panama, western Colombia (Golfo de Cupica), northern Colombia on the Caribbean coast, Venezuela, Guyana, Bolivia, Paraguay, northern Argentina, Parana province of Brazil.

Habitat: This large macaw species (it is only an insignificant bit smaller than the Hyacinth Macaw) almost always lives under 1500 m (4900 ft) in altitude. It lives with the Scarlet Macaw in tropical,

Green-Winged Macaw, *Ara chloroptera*. Green-Winged Macaws have an exceptionally large beak in comparison to the other macaws. They can do a great deal of damage if left unsupervised.

low-lying virgin forests with an average altitude of 300 m (985 ft). In the last decade the Macaw population has retreated from the coastal areas into the interior, avoiding the human settlements.

They rarely live in flocks, mostly living in groups of four to six individuals, or in pairs. River valleys, humid/hot forests, river deltas with expansive swamps, and palm groves form their feeding and nesting areas. With their huge beaks, these birds easily open hard-shelled seeds; the following hard-shelled fruits are most commonly sought after by

this species: *Hymenaea spec., Endopleura uchi*, and *Bertholletia excelsa*.

Green-winged Macaws found in Chaco, Paraguay, and Argentina (Formosa) are probably only seasonal residents.

In the southernmost part of the range of these birds they breed in the months of November/December, while the northernmost population breed in February/March. They make their nests in holes in the trunks of trees, and in holes that they have dug out of the walls of cliffs. The female lays up to two eggs (50 x 35 mm/2 x 1.5 in.) and broods them alone

for about 28 days. The young birds are fed by both parents for 90 to 100 days, and remain in the care of their family for some time afterwards.

Status: As early as 1575 this species was described by the Swiss Naturalist Gessner. It is unknown whether the species was being kept by Europeans at that time. It has been kept for the last hundred years. Presently, this bird is among the most commonly imported of the macaw species, along with *A. ararauna*, and *A. macao*. It is also beloved in its own homeland as a domesticated bird.

"This splendidly feathered bird is much treasured as a house pet by the natives. Its nesting tree is a family possession, and is passed along from generation to generation. The attractive tail and flight feathers are plucked at regular intervals, and serve as ornaments and exchange objects for the owners" (Lantermann).

The first Green-winged Macaw was probably imported to Europe in the beginning of the 17th century. They soon had the reputation as being lovable room companions, and quite able speakers. Their great stature, handsome plumage, and interested personalities quickly made this species a treasured part of the zoological gardens and bird parks. Kept individually, the bird becomes uncommonly tame, and regards its keeper as if he were a feathered companion. Keeping this bird individually is, nevertheless, problematic.

Hoppe describes his own bird: "This author kept a hand-tame Green-winged Macaw in an aviary with Blue and Gold Macaws, Scarlet Macaws, and a Buffon's Macaw. The Green-winged Macaw was the quieting element in the small group. Whenever a quarrel would develop between the other occupants of the aviary over a piece of apple or a better sitting spot, this peacemaker would move between the arguing birds, and managed to quiet the quarrel every time. He enthusiastically presented his head, belly or underside of his wings to be scratched. When he had enough of being scratched, which rarely happened, he carefully took the person's finger in his massive beak, and gently pushed the hand aside."

The affection these birds show for their keepers seems to be a result of their instinctive attachment to their partners. A. Brehm corroborates this point in particular: "As with all parrots, the macaws are loyal spouses. In the month of April, 1788," Azara tells us, "hunter Manuel Palomares, a mile from the city of Paraguay, shot a macaw, and fastened it to the saddle on his horse. The spouse of this bird followed the hunter into the middle of the Capital, to his house, where upon the bird threw itself onto the body of its dead spouse, and stayed several days in the same spot, finally allowing itself to be captured. The bird was kept in the house as a captive resident."

"We hear of similar reports from other researchers. The bonding between two macaw mates is so outstanding that one might say that they live for each other and their broods. This mutual attachment is so well-known in Brazil that hunters use it to trap more of these birds. When one bird has been shot, its mate will appear on the scene almost immediately to find out what has happened to its mate, and its shrieks attract other pairs of birds" (1926).

Humbolt knows of Green-winged Macaws kept as housepets in their homeland: "We were fascinated to see tame Macaws around the huts of the Indians, which flew back and forth to the field, as we might see pigeons in our area. These birds are used as large ornaments in Indians' chicken yards; lacking nothing in splendor to the peacock, gold pheasant, or tree hen.

As early as Columbus, it seems the natives of these areas were raising parrots and other birds in hen houses; Columbus had observed, by the time he discovered America that the natives of the Antilles kept Macaws and other large parrots instead of chickens."

The psychological study by A. Gemein, 1979 on his Green-winged Macaws illuminates the lovable nature of this bird: "The birds are named Sabine and Sebastian. They were bought in Blickfeld together, and are inseparable. With lengths of over 90 cm (36 in.) each, these birds are difficult to ignore. They are constnatly in motion, always occupied in trying to enlarge their quarters, always quick to aggressively investigate their surroundings. Contact with other birds of their species they basically avoid. Sabine, I would describe as moody, stormy, uninhibited, and reckless; Sebastian gives off an air of dignity, maturity and constancy.

The third of this species, although by no means the least, is Bubi. In his care, I've emphasized patience, and sensitivity to his personality. He is perhaps a bit too elegant, or arrogant, maybe even somewhat snooty, and I'm a bit prejudiced against him."

J.S. Rigge achieved the first successful captive breeding in 1962, in Millom, England. Matings in 1960 and 1961 produced no results. The first eggs were not brooded. The embryos of the 1961 clutch died before maturing. The successful brood began in April, 1962 in a aviary measuring 5 m (16.5 ft.) long, 2.5 m (8 ft.) wide, and 2 m (6 ft.) high. The bottom of the nest was laid with some peat sod. From three fertilized eggs, two young birds hatched. An inspection of the nest was impossible because the parents were very aggressive towards intruders; the conspicuous quiet of the parents is also noteworthy. The immatures left the nest after about 103 days. The female had not left the nest for five weeks. The male fed the female, and also directly fed the young himself. The birds were raised on sunflower seeds, a little bit of hemp, and spinach leaves. In 15 years, this pair raised 28 young birds.

The first German breeding of pure-blooded Green-winged Macaws hatched in 1970 in Hannover. Two years later there were birds bred in Texas. The youngest of

Scarlet Macaw, *Ara macao.* The Scarlet Macaw is very vividly colored. It is one of the few macaws to have a completely bare facial area.

these three chicks was neglected by the parents after a few days, and was given to a pair of Scarlet Macaws to be raised. The Green-winged Macaws raised the other two chicks without any problems. There was also a breeding in the Bird Park of Metelen, Germany.

The most recent documented mating was conducted by G. Wilking. In May of 1980, the breeder placed a female with a male that he had procured in 1975. The inner aviary measured 1.5 x 2.4 x 2.3 m (5 x 8 x 7.5 ft). The nest was 1 m (3.3 ft) high, and floor area of 55 x 70 cm (22 x 28 in). The entrance had a diameter of 22cm (8.5 in), and was built into the top third of the wall. The floor of the nest was laid with 10 cm (4 in) of sawdust, and peat. After a few days, the well-harmonized pair inspected the nest. After three weeks, they mated. The breeder mentions the following information: The birds mated on the 16th, 22nd, and 26th of June. The first egg was laid on the 29th of June, and the second on the 2nd of July. The eggs were found to be fertilized on the 5th of July. The second inspection on the 8th of July discovered another egg in the nest. All three eggs had been fertilized. On the 26th of July the first chick hatched from an egg that had cracked already and had been "repaired" by the breeder with a piece of tape. A total of two Green-winged Macaws hatched; the third egg was smashed shortly before hatching.

The young birds grew in their first downy feathers after eight days. After two weeks they opened their eyelids. The first feather quills pressed through in their third week of life, and the bills were already dark at the edge of the base. They first showed the red head feathers after five weeks. At this age their tail and wing feathers were about 3 cm (1.2 in) long. They were fully feathered by the 23rd of October, and after 13 weeks in the nest, they left it. Wilking fed the birds sunflower seeds (soaked), milky corn, nuts, fruit of every kind, cream cheese with fruit pieces mixed in, soaked "Zwieback," and chopped egg with vitamins.

In 1975 and 1976 three young Green-winged Macaws hatched in the Wuppertal Zoo. Unfortunately, one of the parents escaped from the zoo.

Extraordinary success was achieved at the Wuppertal Zoo mating a male Blue and Gold Macaw and a female Green-winged Macaw. This pair produced 40 young birds between the years 1963-1980.

The following data (obtained through letters by Hoppe from Dr. Schurer) seems important for similar broods, although pure breeding is always preferred to hybridization: "The average weight of the eggs was 30 g (.96oz). The weight of the chicks was 25 and 26 g(.8 and .84 oz) when they hatched. It was discovered at the San Diego Zoo that the ideal temperature for the birds lies between 32 and 35°C (89.6 and 95°F). With a uniform temperature ascertained, the young birds were kept in a plastic basket in the incubator to allow for proper air-circulation. The temperature was adjusted to 33.5°C (92.3°F), with an 80% humidity. This temperature was found to be best for the digestive processes of the birds; in the lower temperature ranges the birds developed indigestion. They were fed six times between the hours of 6 am and 10 pm, with a pipette for a while. The feed consisted of a cup of crushed wheat, two egg yolks, and two tablespoons of canned milk. These ingredients were stirred together and diluted with water (to a soupy paste) and cooked over a low flame, until it was a complete paste. Cheese and bananas were added to this mixture."

Out of the three young birds of this mating, two lived to be fully-fledged, so that the hand-raising was worth the effort.

SCARLET MACAW

Scientific Name: *Ara macao*, Linne, 1758

Common Names: Scarlet Macaw, and Red and Yellow Macaw

Field Marks: 85-87 cm (33.5-34.3 in)long; scarlet red; flight and wing coverts blue; back, rump and upper tail coverts brighter blue; large wing coverts, and shoulder coverts yellow, with partially blue and green tips; primaries and secondaries blue; under wing coverts red; under tail coverts bright blue; underside of tail orange to brownish; long tail feathers red with blue tips; skin at side of the head entirely unfeathered, a clear flesh color, some birds have been found with lines of tiny red feathers in this region; upper mandible bright horn colored with side of bill darker at the base; lower mandible black; feet gray brown; irises yellow.

Identifying the female: somewhat smaller bill, forehead line a little duller. Immatures have a grayish lower mandible, their bodies are somewhat smaller, they have brown toes and brown irises. Low (1980) also identifies the immatures by the often stronger green color in their wings.

Range: Bolivia, Mexico to Southern Panama, Colombia, Venequela, Guyana, Surinam, Cayenne, Brazil (in the Fortaleza to Mato Grosso region) and the island of Trinidad.

Habitat: This bird is not among the immediately endangered macaw species. In the last decade, however, they have partially retreated from their original range. This seems to be true in the northernmost region: in Veracruz and Oaxaca, Mexico. In some places they seem to have died out completely or only small remainders of their original populations exist.

Their preferred habitats seem to be up to altitudes of 900 m (2900 ft). They build their homes along the rivers in the surrounding swamp forests. These areas have an annual rainfall of 3000 mm (118 in) in the humid South and only 1500 mm (60 in) in the North. In El Salvador they are only found in the unpopulated coastal areas and in the forests around the Lago de Olomega. There the birds' existence has been upset by the chaos of that country's Civil War:

Pretty Bird International's Bread and Muffin mixes are an easy and fun way to feed your birds and still provide wholesome nutrition.

they are utilized by the human population as food.

Hoppe saw Scarlet Macaws in the vicinity of the town of Rio de Jesus: "On several occasions small troops of eight to ten birds flew by. The pairs flew so closely together that they seemed to nearly touch each other. By the afternoon sunlight their red feathers seemed especially bright. It is a beautiful sight, this large parrot in flight: the fantastic coloring of their wings can be fully appreciated."

The natives of the district of Rio Magdalena in N.W. Colombia where the birds are still relatively common, value these birds as domesticated pets. During the rainy season, on the eastern side of the Andes to Santa Cruz in Bolivia, the Scarlet Macaw lives in forests along the rivers, and in Venezuela, Guyana, Surinam, French Guinea, and Brazil up to an altitude of 1000 m (3200 ft). They avoid human settlements in these areas. They are very shy, and have learned through years of being hunted to keep a long distance in flight between themselves and humans.

Outside of the breeding season, the Scarlet Macaws are found searching for food in clans or small troops, but also in swarms of up to 30 birds. They have a daily routine: in the early mornings they fly off from their roosts and search among the trees for fruit, nuts, and leaf and flower buds. They are known to occasionally feed in the grain and corn fields, causing quite a bit of damage. At midday the

Scarlet Macaw, *Ara macao*, with Walnut. The beaks of macaws are so powerful that they have no trouble cracking open a walnut shell. The beak of a macaw can gently peel the skin of a grape or destroy a large branch in a matter of minutes.

Scarlet Macaw, *Ara macao*, eating grape. Grapes tend to be a favorite treat among macaws. Very often, trainers use grapes as a reward to the bird after it has performed a desired act.

birds sit among shady branches napping and preening.

In the late afternoon, they return to their roosts, where the pairs sit beside one another, caring for each other's feathers and quarrelling with other birds over the best roosts. Up to 30 can lie between their feeding spots and their roosts, which are effortlessly spanned in their rapid flight.

They probably never search the ground for food, although they have been known to pick mineral-rich dirt up along the river banks. P. Roth writes of his 1978 observations: he saw a pair of macaws regularly visit a tree-hole, probably

intending to eat the 10 cm (4 in) long beetle larvae (*Lamellicornia*) that live in the rotted wood: he found no eggs or chicks in the hole. The macaws may have needed the animal protein to feed their young.

Brood holes are often found in dead palm trees. The mates are not the only ones interested in the nesting spots: the native people consider these family possessions and even bequeath them through the generations. Nest holes have also been found along river banks. The slippery banks seem to be good protection against nest plundering mammals.

In the southern part of their range, the Scarlet

Macaw breeds in December, while in the northern zones, the breeding period begins in the months of March/April. Two to four eggs are laid, measuring 47 x 34 mm (2 x 1.3 in). The hen lays the eggs as many as three to five days apart, beginning her clutch as soon as the first egg is laid, so that the last chick to hatch can be as many as two weeks younger than the first hatched. The local people frequently discover new nests, which are visible by the long tail feathers of the brooding bird hanging out of the nest. They often take the young birds out of the nests, raise them by hand, and keep them as house pets. For some tribes, the Scarlet Macaws serve as valuable items of barter; the colorful ornamental feathers are valued. The macaw has been kept domestically as early as the Incan civilization.

Status: The Scarlet Macaw was as common a bird in European homes and zoos as were the Green-winged and Blue and Gold Macaws. Fifteenth and sixteenth century sea-faring Spaniards travelling from Central America brought these splendid birds back with them. They spread in popularity among the royal houses of the time. They were known for the ease with which they were tamed, and their astonishing imitative abilities.

Scarlet Macaw, *Ara macao*. Using a foot to hold food and the other to stand on a perch is no problem for a macaw.

Scarlet Macaw, *Ara macao*. Macaws require perches that are made from strong wood and that have at least 1¼ in diameter. The feet of a macaw should not wrap around completely, the nails should touch the wood so that they can be naturally worn down.

Shown in zoological gardens, in the company of larger, more colorful macaws, they were enthusiastically received by the public. Their agility, loud and varied noises, and the singular attachment the mated birds have for each other are all quite impressive. The Scarlet Macaw should never be kept in temperatures lower than 15°C (59°F), even when it seems able to tolerate short spells of lower temperatures. The practice of keeping these handsome birds locked to foot chains should have been abolished; unfortunately one still sees this highly questionable handling method.

Because of their innate sociability, the Scarlet Macaw can be kept in small swarms with other birds of the species, given enough room. This is also the best way to encourage pairing for breeding.

L.H. Chamness of California is considered the first to have bred this species in captivity in 1916. His pair raised a total of nine broods. Although a clutch can often consist of up to four eggs, generally three young birds are raised. Lord Lilfors of England kept a pair of birds in free flight that bred in 1934 and 1939 and raised the young

in a nest built outdoors. In subsequent years there have been numerous Scarlet Macaws bred in captivity in zoos, parks, and in private hands. With proper handling this does not seem to be a difficult bird to breed.

In 1980, the Fuhs bred the first Scarlet Macaws in Germany. They purchased two macaws that were standing next to each other in their cage, and seemed to have a liking for one another. In February the distinctly smaller hen laid two eggs that unfortunately had not been fertilized. They were kept in an indoor aviary measuring 1.5 x 2.5 x 2.5 m (5 x 8 x 8 ft), with a nest 55 x 55 x 110 cm (22 x 22 x 43in). She laid another two eggs in April of the same year and after 25 days, two chicks hatched. The first of these immediately died. The female kept the remaining chick in the nest for another 60 days, and was an exemplary mother. The pair ate sunflower seeds, cembra-pine nuts, peanuts, carrots, grapes, and oranges. They would not eat the mixture of baby food and "Zwieback," intended for the new birds.

Notable dates in the bird's growth: Day 3: yellow downy plumage. Day 17: the first quills poked through, the chick has tripled in size. Day 42: the first colored feathers are recognizable on the rump, head and wings. Day 49: the colored wing feathers are present. Day 70: more down apparent on rump, breast and belly. Day 105: the immature is fully feathered, but somewhat smaller than its parents. At 90 days the young was seen poking its head out of the nest, interested in the world around it. Around this time the parents took distinctly less food to the nest; it is assumed that the chick stopped growing as rapidly and needed less food. After 105 days of life, the immature left the nest. Problems arose with the birds and the neighbors. The breeder tried to keep the birds quiet, and was moderately successful due to the trusting relationship he had established with the birds.

There was a pair of Scarlet Macaws being kept at the Jerome-Buteyn Bird Ranch in San Luis Rey, California. They were living in a large aviary with other species. The entire aviary was placed at their disposal, however, when they showed signs of mating. The clutch had three eggs, and that same number of birds was raised by the parents. The adults also fed on bread, tomatoes, fruit and chalk (calcium). Shortly before the immatures left the nest they weighed more than the adult birds. "A few days after leaving the nest their weight dropped 10%, so that they averaged from 650 to 800 grams (21 to 25.7 oz" (Lantermann, 1984).

Hybrids between Scarlet Macaws, and other Macaws species are known: A. macao X A. ararauna, in the Krefeld Zoo (two young were raised in a general volary in 1973. In coloring, they were a cross between their two parents); A. macao X A. chloroptera; A. macao X A. ambigua.

There is apparently a common crossbreed known in the U.S.A. as the "Catalina Macaw" (Decoteau, 1982).

Note: At the 5th Conference on the 22nd of April, 1985, held in Buenos Aires, the Scarlet Macaw was reclassified from Appendum II to Appendum I of the Washington Species protection list.

RED-SHOULDERED MACAW
Scientific Name: *Diopsittaca nobilis*, Linne, 1758 (according to Wolters, 1975); *Ara nobilis* (according to Forshaw, 1973).

Common name: Noble Macaw, Hahn's Macaw

The newly designated genus, *Diopsittaca*, is still today classified in different ways. Not only De Grahl like Forshaw, 1974, uses the species name *Ara nobilis*, but also Lantermann; although in his standard work he adopts the classification of Wolters, 1975, unequivocally designating the Red-shouldered Macaw in the genus *Diopsittaca*. Hoppe uses the new classification in 1983, and refers the reader to the following distinction: the bare facial skin on the *Diopsittaca*, unlike the *Ara*, only extends around the eyes and lore region (this is also true for Spix's Macaw, *Cyanopsitta spixii*). *Diopsittaca* is also noticeably smaller than the species in the genus *Ara*. Hoppe suggests for these reasons that the genus *Diopsittaca* can be thought of as an intermediate genus between *Ara* and the genus *Aratinga*.

There are three sub-species:

(1) *Diopsittaca nobilis nobilis* (Linne). Red-shouldered Macaw, Hahn's Macaw.

Field Marks: 30 cm (11.8 in) long; general plumage green; lower breast and belly more of a yellow-green; bend of wing, carpal edge, and underwing coverts red; outer webs of the outermost secondaries blue; underside of wing and tail yellow-green; tail green; crown and forehead bluish; eye region and lore stripes white, almost bare; bill gray-black; feet dark gray; irises orange brown. The head of the female seems smaller and thinner. The forehead and crown coloring is green on immature birds, and the red on the carpal edge, bend of wing, and underwing coverts is less pronounced.

Range: Eastern Venezuela, Guyana, Brazil (Roraima, Para, Amapa).

(2) *Diopsittaca nobilis cumanensis* (Lichtenstein), Noble Macaw.

Field Marks: Similar to *D.n. nobilis*, but noticeably larger; upper mandible horn-colored, with a somewhat darker tip, lower mandible dark gray.

Range: The Brazilian provinces of Para, Maranhao, Piaui, West Pernambuco, Bahia, and Northern Goias.

(3) *Diopsittaca nobilis longipennis* (Neumann). Long-winged Macaw, Neumann's Macaw.

Field Marks: Like *D.n. cumanensis*, but larger.

Range: Brazil (E. Mato Grosso, S. Goias, Minas Gerais, W. Espirito Santo, N. Sao Paulo).

Habitat: In their homeland, the Red-shouldered Macaw lives in tropical regions at altitudes up to 500 m (1600 ft). All three sub-species live in nomadic swarms. It is thought to be quite common in eastern and north eastern South America. They resemble the *Aratinga* species in their behavior, who also live gregariously in swarms. Their characteristic call, given during flight, serves to keep families and mates together, as is true for the *Aratinga*.

Tropical coastal forests, open palm groves, and even areas around the cities serve as habitats for this bird. Hoppe described in his stay in Georgetown being awakened regularly by the cries of the Red-shouldered Macaw.

It is not certain whether birds of this genus form the lifelong mates as do the larger species. They first pair off at the beginning of the breeding season, and make their nests mainly in palm trees. Eggs and young birds have also been found in the constructions of tree-inhabiting termites.

Status: The sub-species *D.n. cumanensis* was first kept in Europe in the London Zoo in 1872, and was first seen in the Berlin Zoo in 1915. The Red-shouldered Macaw species never attained the popularity that their larger cousins have. Their plumage is relatively unspectacular by comparison, and their cries are too distracting for most cage or aviary keepers. When kept individually they have certainly delighted keepers with increasing tameness, devotion, and imitative abilities. A woman from Proschek, Vienna, reports that her bird had learned 50 words. Russ, as early as 1882, praised this species: "Tameness, and liveliness." The Red-shouldered Macaw has not always been recognized as a macaw by zoos.

Newly imported birds should be accommodated under careful temperature control. It should not drop below 10°C (50°F). A cabinet with separate sleeping and roosting chambers under each other is suggested.   Should one desire to keep a pair of this species inside, one need not buy as large a cage as you would for the larger macaws. It is better to make flight room available: *D. nobilis* is considered one of the best fliers of the macaws. They can also be kept in small swarms, which best suit their sociable nature. Unfortunately, the Red-

shouldered Macaw has a tendency to pluck its feathers when kept in a cage.

The first captive breeding was registered in the U.S.A. in 1939. Three young *D.n. cumanensis* were hand-raised. We know more of the successful breeding by E.N.T. Vane: a female *D.n. cumanensis* brooded four eggs for 25 days in 1949. The young left the nest after two months. The pair raised a total of 30 young from 1949 to 1956.

The first German breeding occurred in 1963 in the small Hof Zoo. They were first reported as Chestnut-fronted Macaws (*A. severa*), however, Hoppe suggests this was an error. The pair was kept in an aviary measuring 3 x 3 x 2.5 m (10 x 10 x 8 ft), with an inner chamber 3 x 2 x 1.5 m (10 x 6 x 5 ft). The nest measured 30 x 30 x 70 cm (12 x 12 x 28 in), but the birds became disinterested in it after a time. Instead they escaped through a board that they had gnawed through, and in vain laid three eggs on the wooden floor of a hay loft. Afterwards, in the same attic, she again laid three eggs, out of which one young hatched. The nesting time was estimated at three months, but it is not certain.

In 1975, De Grahl kept four birds of the nominal form. Two of the birds paired off and were placed in a room measuring 1 x 1 x 2.3 m (3.3 x 3.3 x 7.5 ft)for breeding. The male had a wider shaped head, a stouter build, and the bare facial area was more extensive on him. The female brooded four eggs, alone in March, during which time the male was only sporadically seen inside the nest. After the young hatched on the 1st of April, the pair was quite aggressive. Besides two unfertilized eggs, one immature was found in the nest. Regarding their development: at 10 days, the eyes were still shut; at 20 days, the eyelids had opened, and dark quills could be seen under the skin. The first feathers emerged on the wings and tail after 30 days, and the bird weighed 150 g (5 oz.) at this time; after six weeks, its body weight was registered at 180 g (5.7 oz.), its bill was horn-colored and its irises clear brown. By the time it left the nest it had lost about 20 g (.64 oz.) and its bill was gray colored. The immature left the nest at exactly 60 days old "accompanied by the excited cries of its parents." After another two weeks, it fed itself. Before that its parents had fed it cooked sunflower seeds, grated carrots, and egg food.

Green Winged Macaw, *Ara chloroptera*. Indeed the macaws are capable of inflicting serious wounds if handled improperly, but for the most part they are docile, gentle birds that will not bite unless provoked.

Keeping a Macaw

ADVICE ON BUYING A BIRD

1. Discuss and consider among family members whether the keeping and handling of a bird is sensible and feasible.

2. Make a preliminary decision as to which species of bird should be sought, based on size, imitative abilities, and coloration.

3. Look at a large selection of birds. Do not settle for the only bird available.

4. Look for a young bird. They can be identified by: dark irises, faded plumage coloring, and finely scaled feet and toes.

5. Ask about the feed that the bird is used to eating.

6. Look for a healthy shine in the bird's eyes. The bird should also exhibit the following qualities:

a) smooth, evenly laid plumage, especially on the head and neck.

b) open, clear eyes, blinking alertly, not apathetic.

c) full sets of claws, and an undamaged bill.

d) clear nostrils, not stopped up.

The following can indicate a sick bird:

1. Sudden opening of the beak that looks like the bird is yawning;

2. Smacking noises as it opens and closes its beak;

3. Audible inhaling and exhaling, with its tail feathers raising and falling, called "difficult breathing";

4. Runny or foamy dung;

5. Constantly standing on the bottom of the cage, or aviary with ruffled feathers;

6. Bloody or freshly scabbed wounds on its wings indicating an inexperienced wing clipper. All newly imported birds have had their flight feathers clipped; these will grow back in the next molting season.

ADVICE ON ACCOMMODATION AND CARE

1. Obtain the largest possible cage, with square corners (never round cages) and cross bars that are of neither too thick nor too thin, rounded wood. Swinging stands are inappropriate in the beginning.

2. The cage should be

placed out of drafts with either one or two sides against the wall. It should be approximately chest high, and should sit neither in the direct sunlight nor in the dark.

3. The cage should have a sturdy door lock that the bird cannot open on its own. The food dishes should be securely attached, though removable.

4. It is not recommended that birds be kept on stands with foot chains, although with proper care, and laying of the chain, partly tamed birds can be further trained by this means. Utmost care should be taken to prevent the bird from hurting or even hanging itself. One should also build additional climbing places for the bird.

5. The bird should occasionally be taken outside, on a balcony or in a garden for some fresh air, care being taken that the bird does not escape.

6. Birds should be watched attentively when let out into rooms. They love to chew on wood, rugs, books, and curtains. Care should also be taken against electrocution from chewing on electrical cords.

7. These species are most content when kept in pairs or small groups in aviaries. In the wintertime they need a lightly heated draft-free inner chamber.

ADVICE ON FEEDING

BASIC FEED

Sunflower seed, hemp (very little), canary seeds, all types of millet, wheat, corn, rice, hazel nuts, walnuts, peanuts, cembra-pine nuts, Brazil nuts.

SUPPLEMENTS

"Zwieback", white bread, dates, figs, cooked rice, pumpkin seeds, chestnuts, acorns, beechnuts.

BRANCHES

Linden, poplar, willow, birch, fruit (non-toxic), non-toxic pine trees.

FRESH FOODS

Fruit

Apples, pears, bananas, peaches, plums, grapes, oranges, cherries, pineapples, raisins.

Vegetables

(No cabbage!), corn cobs, carrots, rosehips, rowan berries, elder berries, raw oats and wheat.

Other

Cooked poultry, veal, cooked fish, raw and

Feather plucked Scarlet Macaw, *Ara macao*. It is generally agreed that feather plucking arises from boredom, stress, or lack of a varied diet. It becomes a behavioral problem that usually can not be corrected.

cooked bones, grape sugar, mussel shells, and egg shells.

VITAMINS
A, D3, E1, B-complex, K.

MINERALS AND TRACE ELEMENTS
Iron, copper, chlorine, manganese, magnesium, phosphorus, sulfur, iodine, sodium, silicon, sugar, pectin, processed honey, parrot feed in pellet form.

Fresh drinking water is very important, and weak tea is also good. No coffee or alcohol, and be careful not to overdose the birds on store-bought liquid vitamins!

These birds also need baths two to three times a week with a fine-spray watering can and lukewarm water. Their cages should be cleaned regularly and fresh mineral-rich bottom sand should be added (this can be bought already prepared). Their claws should be clipped as needed (only within 2 mm (.1 in) of their veins).

ADVICE ON TAMING
1. The new bird should be left quietly in its cage for a few weeks, until it has become accustomed to being alone, and to its new environment.

2. When cleaning its cage or filling its feed and water trays, the bird should be approached quietly with the keeper speaking softly, and these tasks being cautiously executed. (Under no circumstances should the bird ever be chased around the cage as it tries to fly off from your hands.)

3. Teach the bird to be hand-fed. By and by you can try reaching tidbits (like fresh corn, shelled sunflower seeds, spray millet and peanuts) through the bars. The bird will probably not accept these at first, but should be continually offered these, especially when it is hungry. One should speak softly to the bird while attempting to feed it, so that it gets used to its keeper's voice.

4. Care should be taken when reaching into the cage to feed the bird. After a while the forefinger can be reached under the bird's feet as it sits, and bit by bit pushed under its toes, until the bird remains perched on the finger. When the bird has confidence in your hand, and will perch on it in the cage, the bird can be carefully taken out of the cage, and after a short time, placed on top of the cage.

5. Feather scratching: A bird will generally allow the

human hand near its head after it has learned to sit on a finger. With an outreached finger, one must try to scratch the bird on its head. This is the manner in which birds socialize among themselves. He will begin to enjoy it and eagerly allow himself to be scratched.

TEACHING TO SPEAK

The following distinctions are made among imitative achievements:
1. Simple sound imitation.
2. Transposition and variation.
3. Sound emission related to situations.
4. Using "Speech" to satisfy needs.
5. Anticipating or wanting responses by speaking.

The imitative abilities of the macaw, as with all "speaking" birds, happen because they can learn to produce sounds other than those in their instinctive repertoire. They are actually so intelligent that they are thought to be able to imitate in order to affect and improve their living situation and social relations. My assumption (1979) is corroborated by Bosch/Wedde in their volume *Amazons* (1981).

The following guidelines are valuable for the gradual speech "instruction" of a Macaw:

1. The bird should be approached when it is in a quiet frame of mind, when it is sitting quietly in its cage or on your hand, looking interested. Evenings seem to be a good time for this.

2. Choose a name for the bird that uses sounds natural to it (for example "Gurri," "Koko," "Lina," etc.).

3. Repeat the bird's name to it steadily, in not too deep a voice, carefully pronouncing the consonants.

4. Gradually expand its vocabulary with new words, so that it will retain the first words that it learns.

5. The time the bird takes to learn to imitate will depend on how tame it is. It can take six to eight weeks for the bird to learn to trust its keeper, although some birds may be reproducing sounds in just a few months. Some birds prefer whistles and melodies to spoken words. Fully accomplished speakers are rare.

As the bird learns more of the human sounds that surround it, it will begin to abandon its loud and somewhat disruptive natural tones. Each bird's accomplishments will depend on its innate abilities, and the degree to which it has bonded with its keeper.

ADVICE ON PROBLEMS
Screeching

In its natural habitat, birds' cries serve to keep the groups together, warn of approaching enemies, and the expression of any irregularities. At first solitary birds will call for their missing comrades. As the bird learns to imitate its surroundings and human speech, and as it has more contact with its keeper, these screeches will subside, although rarely will they stop completely.

Should the bird become really troublesome and loud, the best means of quieting it seems to be by quiet contact and talking to it. In the morning and late afternoons one might feel the need to "raise one's hand," to get a word in edgewise. One should not meet the bird's noises with louder sounds: vacuum cleaners, engine noises, loud music, etc.

Other steps one might take to end the screeching: One can rebuild what may have become an uncomfortable, worn-out perch, out of natural materials: wood, branches, etc. More climbing spots can be added onto the bird's perch. One can try to startle the bird out of its screaming pattern by quickly darkening the room. After a quiet evening, however, one should leave the room light on a while so the bird can take its nightly roost.

Feather Plucking

Feather chewing and plucking most often indicate a psychological disturbance. Perhaps boredom, lack of exercise, loss of the bird's comrades, the inability to fly after its wings have been clipped, or a poor relationship with its keeper all contribute to this behavior. The "psychological needs" of the bird compel it to bite off or rip out its feathers, or to tear at its skin and muscle. Effective measures against this seem to be: increased contact and interest on the part of the bird's keeper; the companionship of another bird of its own species, or even another parrot; some of the measures mentioned under "screeching" might be tried and more variety in its feed, and more time out of its cage.

Special sprays are also available that, while non-toxic, give the feathers a bitter flavor, and discourage this behavior.

Breeding

Captive breeding of the Macaw seems a sensible endeavor for countless reasons. First of all, keeping the birds in pairs or groups fills the need they have for company. Problems associated with keeping individual birds can be alleviated, or even completely avoided. Keeping the birds in pairs for breeding also means that they are not being kept on chains, which has been a cruel reality in the past of large parrots, and birds of every species. The large aviaries that have room for the birds to fly (both inside and out) are a more equitable manner of keeping birds than are the small cages that give the bird no room for flight.

Furthermore, mated birds have an opportunity to express their instinctive social nature, and the related signals (shape, color, gestures, vocal emissions, and total expressive behaviors) they can "hang out" with one another in all the positive senses. Finally, observation of the pair and of the hopefully successful breeding of the birds gives the bird enthusiast an incomparable opportunity to indulge his/her ornithological and ecological interests.

It should also be mentioned that the passionate amateur who keeps macaws and breeds them, can make worthwhile contributions to scientific knowledge of the bird's reproductive biology, and can contribute to the protection of this handsome bird.

These are all good reasons for keeping the macaw in pairs rather than individually, when possible. It should also be mentioned that by planned breeding, the quotas for birds captured in the wild could be lowered, and even species whose existence is not threatened in their natural habitat could be spared.

Eventually, it would seem ideal that macaw species in their natural habitats be spared to the point that no birds at all are captured. On the other hand, keeping and observing the socially developed macaw is a sensible and important endeavor for the nature-conscious individual, breeding being an integral part of this.

Successful breeding depends on adequate

knowledge. While it seems evident that this bird will breed when kept in large aviaries, it has also been known to mate in cages that seem small in proportion to the size of the birds. An outdoor flight-aviary, built onto a concrete slab, is most appropriate, keeping the birds from flying off, and from escaping by digging through a dirt floor. The birds are thus kept in near natural conditions, regarding ventilation, rain, sunshine, and a summertime temperature over 20°C (68°F), resembling the environment in their natural habitat. Light, oxygen, and moisture are essential to the regulation of the bird's metabolism, nervous system and behavior. As natural an environment as is possible is essential to encourage the birds to breed.

The inner chamber of the aviary should give the birds a draft-free, warm area when the temperature drops, that allows for the bird's flight, and protects from direct sunlight.

The nest-hole should resemble a natural brooding area as much as possible: a hollowed-out tree trunk 80-100 cm (31.5-39.5in) high, and an inner breadth of 30-50 cm (12-20 in) in diameter is preferred to crates, or plastic barrels, although the latter have produced successful broods. The nest should be lined with layer of wood chips and coarse sawdust. On the side, 15 cm (6 in) above the floor, there should be an unlocked flap, through which the eggs and chicks can be inspected. Some

Scarlet macaw, *Ara macao*, and Blue and Gold, *Ara ararauna*. Macaws should be housed in large cages and roomy aviaries to prevent tail damage.

breeders have suggested narrowing the nest entry—which may have a diameter of 10-20 cm (4 -8 in.) depending on the species—with soft wood; working to widen the entrance seems to stimulate the birds to mate.

Another prerequisite for a successful reproduction is a harmonious pair of birds. As with all large parrots, and some parakeet species, macaws form friendships based on their own criteria, i.e. the mates must first "find each other," and then establish their almost human dedication to each other. If it is economically possible, and spatially feasible, keeping four or more birds together will improve the chances that a harmonious pair will establish itself in a relatively short period of time. With some luck, and proper accommodations, it is possible to find a pair of birds who will have an instant liking for each other.

Recognizing the sex of a

macaw can be a problem. As with the individually described species, the experienced breeder can, with some degree of certainty distinguish the majority of birds based on the lengths of the body, head, bill and feathers, as well as the general plumage color, and other colorations. These distinctions are never beyond doubt, however; there have been breeders with supposed males that have laid eggs, or birds who have exhibited different markings, and acted like mating couples, who have turned out to be two males, practicing homosexual love. As a rule, mating macaw males have an unmistakeably impressive carriage. They dance around the hens on the branch, flapping their wings.

Obviously, birds chosen for mating must be of a suitable age. Macaws generally do not mate before their fifth year of life. Lantermann writes that the smaller species will mate in their third or fourth year.

The onset of the breeding instinct is also contingent on the time of large feather molting, and the climate in which they are being kept. Birds kept in this climate breed perennially, when they have molted out well. Even birds who have been kept for many years individually in cages, that seem more human than bird-like are suitable in many cases to be bred.

If one needs absolute certainty as to the sex of his/her bird, a veterinarian can examine the bird endoscopically. Through an illuminated tube, inserted into a small incision under the left wing of an anesthetized bird, an expert can ascertain the sex of the bird. Other methods include examination of the bird's dung (determining the estrogen or testosterone levels), and microscopic examination of the feathers. There is also research being done studying the differences in blood chromosomes. The best method of pairing off birds still seems to be the bird's own choice.

When the days get longer in April and May, the macaw pairs will become interested in mating. The birds become interested both in each other— perceptibly less in their mating rituals than in their mutual preening—and in their nest. Moreover, one should hang a number of nests in different places around the roofed inner aviary, allowing the pair to

Baby Scarlet Macaw, *Ara macao*. Domestically bred macaws are quite expensive but are well worth the money. Breeders are often limited in the number of hand-reared young they can sell because of the limited breeding stock they have.

choose their nest. The others can be removed when the birds have been repeatedly seen inspecting one particular nest, largely ignoring the others. Having once chosen their nest, the pair will always return to the spot to nest.

The male feeding the female is a certain sign of impending mating and the beginning of a brood, although weeks, even months can follow before there is any more progress. If other birds of the species are being kept in the same room, a situation which promotes the forming of pairs, the other birds should be removed to another aviary, so that the mating birds can further prepare themselves for their broods.

The aviary should be approached as little as possible in this period; strangers should not approach the birds at all so as not to unnecessarily disturb the birds. They are best observed at this time through a small observation window in the door. Even entry by keepers of the larger macaws is not without risks—these birds can be extremely aggressive, and have been known to inflict severe bites with their powerful beaks.

If there are no disruptions, and the feed is

right (there should be a good variety of food: fruit, sprouts, vitamin-rich soft-feed and water), then at the end of three or four weeks of courting, the birds should copulate; they will probably engage repeatedly in this.

After three days, the macaw hen will lay her eggs, which are always pure white, as are those of any cave or hole-nesting species. As a rule, the male will attend to the female during her clutch, moving about her, feeding her out of his crop, and keeping watch at the entrance to the nest. A bird keeper would do well to be especially cautious of the male's strong beak at this time. The clutch will incubate between 24 and 28 days depending on the species; it can consist of up to four eggs (*Diopsittaca nobilis*) mostly ranging between two and three eggs.

After the young have hatched, the feed mixture becomes even more important. Partially germinated sunflower seeds, and milky corn on the cob, are good basic feed. Then, depending on their custom and tastes, the parents will take their young lots of ripe fruit, chopped egg, and store-bought mixtures softened with cheese curds. The average nesting period lasts 12 weeks. The female is not obliged to raise the young alone; the male participates at first by feeding the female and then later by also feeding the young.

After the immatures have left the nest, they will continue to be fed by their parents for several weeks. After a time, the parents will bite the young if they approach, and they remain independent of one another, however, staying within sight of their parents, thereby insuring the behavioral patterns specific to each species.

Artificial incubation and hand-raising require quite a bit of trouble and expertise. If a natural brood for some reason is not possible, however, one should try to get the healthy eggs into an incubator. It doesn't matter whether the eggs are freshly laid, or had been brooded, and were abandoned, although abandoned eggs should not be too cool when placed in the incubator. An embryo can occasionally survive long after it has been regarded as dead.

The temperature in an incubator must be at least 38.5°C (101.3°F), with a relative humidity from 70-80%. The eggs need to be turned twice daily. Towards the end of the brood, the humidity should be raised, better enabling the chicks to get through the shell.

When these "incubator chicks" have hatched, they will not need food for 10-12 hours; up to this time they have been nourished by their egg yolk. The freshly hatched young must be kept in a container at 32-35°C (89.6-95°F), with a soft padding underneath them. Little by little the temperature should be lowered, avoding any sudden drops, to keep the young birds from developing indigestion.

For the first three to four weeks, the young macaws need to be fed every two to three hours (throughout the first few nights as well, after which they need not be fed between 10 pm and 6 am). A runny, easily digestible mash, put into a disposable syringe (no needle!) should be trickled into the young birds' throats—otherwise they will choke. The crop should not be too full after feeding—the amount that the birds eat will depend on their age.

Hoppe suggests the following mixture: "cup of wheat grits with two egg yolks mixed with two tablespoons of canned milk and a bit of water to a soupy paste. This paste should be cooked over a low flame, until it begins to firm. After cooling, cheese curds and bananas should be added in the following proportions: $6/8$ paste, $1/8$ banana, and $1/8$ curds. To this mixture add: soft, half ripe Maize (where available), sprouted grains, and a few oil-rich seeds. One can also add alternating vitamin preparations. The birds' calcium needs can be filled by adding small amounts of grated chalk. The feed should be warmed to the birds' body temperature. There are, naturally, other appropriate feeds and mixtures.

Using a disposable plastic syringe with a thin soft tube over the end, instead of the needle, the birds' feed can be squirted through the beak directly into the crop. This procedure should only be attempted by an experienced bird-handler: the bird would be instantly killed should the feed be put into the windpipe instead of the esophagus. One should keep to this rather time-consuming method of trickling the feed into the birds' throat for as long as possible, later feeding with a laterally creased spoon.

Hand-raising a young

Macaw requires considerable dedication; the nesting period, until the bird can feed independently, can last three to four months. If the raising is successful, the breeder can pride himself in the fully tamed and devoted bird. A bird, however, that will be extremely dependent on humans for the rest of its life. Problems often arise when these birds are placed in the company of others of their species. There are a few known cases of human-raised birds who have later lived well with their own species.

Suggested Reading

T.F.H. offers the most comprehensive selections of books dealing with pet birds. A selection of significant titles is presented here; they and the hundreds of other animal books published by T.F.H. are available at the same place you bought this one, or write to us for a free catalog.

T.F.H. Publications
One T.F.H. Plaza
Third & Union Avenues
Neptune City, NJ 07753

INDEX

Page numbers in boldface **refer to illustrations.**